Watching Babylon

Most of us experienced the war against Iraq as spectators, watching the conflict on TV, the Internet or in print media. In this urgent and compelling book, Nicholas Mirzoeff examines what it was like to watch the war, and how the visualized nature of the conflict signalled a consolidation of a new kind of globalized power, of which we are all subjects.

Mirzoeff traces connections between the doctrine of pre-emptive attack that justified "the war on terror" and the campaign against Iraq and what he calls "the empire of camps", pre-figured in the network of punitive internment centres, such as those at Guantánamo Bay, Woomera and Belmarsh, where presumed "others" – migrants, refugees and suspected "enemy combatants" – are imprisoned indefinitely, rendered invisible.

Linking three figurations of Babylon – ancient Babylon, in present-day Iraq, the metaphorical Babylon of Western modernity, and everyday life in the modern suburb of Babylon, New York, Mirzoeff shows how the past and its metaphors overlap with and inform the present. Arguing passionately against a neatly divided world and the stark choice of "with us" or "against us" – whether "us" is the United States or al-Qa'ida – he suggests instead alternative ways of living, outside "Babylon" and the empire of camps.

Nicholas Mirzoeff is Professor of Art and Art Professions at New York University. He is the author of *An Introduction to Visual Culture* (1999), and the editor of *The Visual Culture Reader* (second edition 2002).

Watching Babylon

The war in Iraq and global visual culture

Nicholas Mirzoeff

Routledge
Taylor & Francis Group

NEW YORK AND LONDON

First published 2005 in the USA and Canada
by Routledge
711 Third Avenue, New York, NY 10017

Simultaneously published
by Routledge
2 Park Square, Milton Park, Abingdon,
Oxon OX14 4RN

Routledge is an imprint of the Taylor & Francis Group, an informa business

© 2005 Nicholas Mirzoeff

Typeset in Perpetua by
Florence Production Ltd, Stoodleigh, Devon

Index compiled by Indexing Specialists (UK) Limited,
202 Church Road, Hove, East Sussex, BN3 2DJ

British Library Cataloguing in Publication Data
A catalogue record for this book is available
from the British Library

Library of Congress Cataloging in Publication Data

ISBN 10: 0-415-34309-7 (cased)
ISBN 10: 0-415-34310-0 (limp)

ISBN 13: 978-0-415-34309-1 (cased)
ISBN 13: 978-0-415-34310-7 (limp)

Contents

List of figures

Prologue: Babylonian modernity

When the "shock and awe" stage of the invasion of Iraq began, I was watching TV from an exercise bike in a Long Island gym. Like most American gyms, it is arranged so that those performing the mind-numbing tasks of cardio-vascular exercise can distract themselves by staring at televisions. Usually these are tuned to a variety of stations giving the viewer a stroll through the endlessly varied yet endlessly similar world of cable television in America. On this day, all the images were simply the same. Above station identification logos and text descriptors highlighted on brightly colored backgrounds, intense white flashes tinged with orange filled the screens. The high-quality pictures provided by Abu Dhabi television removed the usual sense of distance offered by grainy night-vision shots and the images were truly shocking. Ahead of me was a middle-aged white man pumping an elliptical trainer, wearing what I can only call a Military Metal T-shirt and a brand-new army baseball cap worn backwards. As the exercise soldier cheered each explosion, I realized that his clothes had been bought for watching the war. As I watched him watching, I became aware that I had nothing to say back to him that might deflate his bombast. This was literally the exercise of power. Apart from short comments from the man on the next machine, whom he directly addressed, the TV soldier had the floor to himself. For all the deconstructive, feminist, anti-racist, visual culture theory that I have at my disposal, there was no way to counter the sweating, exulting triumph of the war watcher. To call attention to the deaths of Iraqi civilians or to mention that this attack lacked the authority of the United Nations would simply have added to his delight.

Yet the war was not a new beginning. Like hanging, war concentrates the mind. In this light, the war marks the end of a certain moment in the development of the current form of globalization in which a new visual Tower of Babel fell. This new Babel wanted to make a place for the visual above the plains of the text from which a new view of the world might be had. Like the first tower, it was built from below to challenge the place of High Culture. This spiraling ziggurat was hailed in 1994 by W.J.T. Mitchell as the "pictorial turn," presenting a new challenge to the humanities in general.[1] As digital culture interfaced with globalization, the visual turn promised to be the key location for its interpretation. It seemed that the new hybridity of globalization could be represented in what Sarat Maharaj called "the new international visual Esperanto."[2] Certain possibilities seemed at hand from the displacement of the text as the prime locus of intellectual work to the creation of new post-disciplinary forms of

Figure I.1 Night-time bombing of Baghdad
(Courtesy of REUTERS/Goran Tomasevic)

university teaching, a democratization of visual media and a move towards the emancipation from menial work that cybernetic automation has been promising since the 1950s. It is not my intention to disavow those hopes but rather to suggest that while the visual may be the locus of globalization, it now resists the viewer, rather than being a place where the viewer might resist or refuse that globalization.

This book does not, however, perform that ritual "exposure" of media images of the war as unrepresentative. It is rather concerned with the consolidation of power as a visualized model of reactionary globalization and the place of people as visual subjects within that system. For visual culture concerns itself with what I call visual subjects: people defined as the agents of sight (regardless of their biological capacity to see) and as the objects of certain discourses of visuality. In short, I seek to establish the possibilities for visual subjectivity in everyday life under the conditions of the permanent state of exception established by the war on terror and exemplified by the war in Iraq. This book examines what it means to watch images of the exercise of power on a global scale from specific localities. It takes as its frame the war in Iraq from the beginning of hostilities to the capture of Saddam Hussein, which is used not as marking an end to the fighting, but as a similarly powerful visual symbol as that of the first explosions. Whether the insurgency continues apace or is now to be contained to sporadic incidents, it has become clear that the United States intends to withdraw from the country as soon as possible, beginning in 2004. No doubt surprises are ahead but it is now both possible and necessary to begin the task of rethinking the global imaginary in the light of the Iraq war. This book concentrates on the related questions of watching, the status of the visual event, and the visualized model of power in global culture, without pretending to exhaust all that needs to be said about the war. Its concentration is the visual media, my area of expertise, rather than political or military policy. It has certainly become hard to separate these areas in neat disciplinary fashion but my source material is drawn from the media rather than from government documents or archives, most of which are as yet classified in any event. Rather than try and go "behind" the war image, as exemplified by the political engagement of Noam Chomsky, I examine what it means to watch images of the exercise of power on a global scale from specific localities.

As a citizen of the European Union, who watched the war in the United States, there is no point in denying that mine is a Western viewpoint, as much as I try and disidentify with it. At the same time, this excuse should not be used to contain the analysis of the effects of the war. I approach this problem of framing through the figure of Babylon, which plays the role for me that the Arcades of nineteenth-century Paris performed for the critic Walter Benjamin in his 1930s study of modernity – that is to say, a physical and historical space that is nonetheless profoundly disjunctured and ambiguous, interspersing the contemporary and the future it is trying to dream with the primal past. Situated in the Euphrates river valley, in what is now Iraq, Babylon represents the historical and mythical city that was the site of the Tower of Babel and a key metropolis and sometime capital of the Assyro-Babylonian empire from the twenty-fourth century BCE to the sixth century CE. However, I will use "Babylon" here to refer to the complex cultural resonances implied by the mythic and historical experience that the name implies, rather than in the specific manner of the historian. Babylon is a metaphor for complexity, exile, decadence that has resonated throughout Western modernity as well as the site of a series of historical and mythical experiences. It was the place of exile for the Jews and the imaginary locus of similar displacement for Africans in slavery. The Babylonian captivity of the Jews began with the Babylonian conquest of Jerusalem in 597 BCE, reinforced by a second wave of exiles after the destruction of the Temple by Nebuchadnezzar in 586 BCE, and ended with the capture of the city by Cyrus of Persia in 579. For later writers trying to place Judaism and Christianity in tension as opposites, Babylon was an irritating complication. Most, like Hegel, mentioned it and then ignored the ensuing consequences. For a writer like Matthew Arnold trying to define a tension between the Hebrew and the Greek view of the world, Babylon was an annoying complication that could be forgotten.[3] But it is exactly that sense that Babylon has always been there but refuses to fall into the grand binary schemes that interests me about it. It should be added that al-Hillah, the city nearest to the site of Babylon, was the scene of serious fighting in the First World War, during the brief but violent anti-colonial revolt against the British in 1920 and again in the 2003 invasion.

From this dynamic mixture of myth, history and dream, I have taken several key ideas. In Rastafari, the syncretic popular religion of the Caribbean that has had widespread influence in popular culture through reggae music, Babylon is the figure for global capitalism and its police. So in thinking about the war in Babylon, I have naturally been drawn to reflections on the current state of globalization. As is so often said, the global is known via the local and there is a township called Babylon on Long Island, near where I watched the war. This Babylon is the site of a specific local vernacular watching that addresses the peculiarity of American visual subjectivity. And finally, according to family legend, I am of Babylonian descent, in the sense that my Sephardic Jewish ancestors claimed to have been exiled to Babylon and to have moved from there to Central Asia in more recent times. My investment is everywhere in the book, for better or worse, and is that of a person who was not only passionately against the war but also felt that it marked a transition even as compared with the other wars of emergent globalization in Kosovo, Somalia, Sierra Leone, Indonesia, Chechnya and so on. Babylon is, then, what Walter Benjamin called a "dream image" that makes it possible to think through the tensions and ambiguities it embodies. These include the sense that Babylon is at once the pre-history of the present and a descriptor of the utterly contemporary; that it represents the popular but also autocratic empire; it is the place of exile and the place where the Babylonian Talmud was written that engenders a profound sense of belonging and modernity for writers as distinct as the British novelist of multiculturalism Zadie Smith and Leon Wieseltier, the sage of neo-Judaism.[4] These embodied contradictions form what I call Babylonian modernity, the ruins of the present lying amid pasts that are not yet past and paths to a future that is yet to come.

After the flood

Let's begin at the oldest place to begin again: after the flood. Babel was the city built after the flood that cannot be recuperated into the West's narrative of itself without complicating it. In Genesis, the figure of Nimrod the hunter inexplicably appears after the flood, building Babylon with the help of giants. In fact, the legends of ancient Mesopotamia celebrated this secret knowledge, so that one of Gilgamesh's attributes is that "He brought back a tale of times before the Flood."[5] In a sense, Babylon and its Tower of Babel was the moment of original complication in which the first language gave way to the mutually unintelligible languages of historical time. The hubris of Babel was not just its unification of language but its aspiration to the divine viewpoint, what cultural theorist Donna Haraway calls the "god trick." In this case, God wasn't having it. The Biblical account, early in Genesis, suggests a different relationship of the divine and the human than the omniscience and omnipotence promoted by today's fundamentalisms of all stripes. The builders of Babel wanted to "make ourselves a name" independently of God. God therefore has to "come down" to Babel to discover what the Babylonians are doing and then he disperses them "over the face of all the earth." In that sense, we are all Babylonians. But the brief Biblical account leaves more questions open than it answers. Why did God not know what they were doing? And if Hebrew was the originary language spoken in the Garden of Eden, as Jewish tradition insists, what forbidden language were the Babylonians speaking? It is this indeterminacy that the returning legend of Babylon inserts into the overweening narratives of power and the powerful, even as it is a metaphor for the inevitable decline of empires. Jacques Derrida, the philosopher of deconstruction, has argued that Babel "exhibits an incompletion, the impossibility of finishing, of totalizing, of saturating."[6] That is to say, Babel represents both the first

Figure I.2 Nimrod building Babylon
(Courtesy of The British Museum)

deconstruction and the inevitability of deconstruction, however dominant that which is to be deconstructed may appear.

If the 1990s claimed to see a visual Tower of Babel being built, however optimistically, it was not, like the original tower, destroyed by God but rather by the converging forces of the military-visual complex and the globalized economy. The obverse of its destruction was the 9-11 attack on the World Trade Center, another jealous protest against secular globalization. In Derrida's discussion of what he calls "the jealousy of God," evidenced in the deconstruction of Babel, he finds himself reminded of James Joyce's aphorism in his novel *Finnegan's Wake*: "And he war." And so we war over Babel again. The "he war" has reinstated war as the proper affect of an aggressive heterosexuality that displaced the Babylonian excesses of what queer theorist Judith Halberstam has called the transgender moment of the 1990s. It situated the nation state as the proper arbiter of globalization, especially over the global work-force. "He war" tears down the panopticon as being dangerously close to the Tower of Babel and puts in its stead the invisible camp for refugees or so-called "enemy combatants," such as the appropriately named Camp X-Ray at Guantánamo Bay, Cuba. Flesh is invisible to the he war. The films for these times are those in the *Lord of the Rings* trilogy (2001–2003), in which a Christianized replay of the Second World War sets out to destroy the tower. The exercise soldier I met in Long Island felt himself empowered as visual subject by the sight of Baghdad being bombed, recognizing a "he war" when he saw one. His screen was filled with what Walter Benjamin called the "empty, homogeneous now" of capital in which he felt trapped between the world wars. I see the spectacle created by the war in a different form. This new fall of Babel was an inter-section of past, present and future created by the collisions and dis-ruptions of global capital. For in German, as Joyce knew very well, "war" means "was." In the war, what was is, and will be again. This spectral spectacle is rife with the implications of Babylon.

When rebuilt by Nebuchadnezzar in the sixth century BCE, Babylon declared its own "behold in awe" policy with its magnif-icent decorations, including the dramatic Ishtar Gate to the city now preserved in the Pergamon Museum, Berlin. The gate was sacred to the goddess Ishtar and led to the processional way used on ceremonial occasions. All were decorated with glazed tiles forming intricate floral patterns on a deep blue background and bas-relief animal sculptures of lions, dragons and donkeys. Alongside the gate Nebuchadnezzar placed a cuneiform inscription declaring his role in creating the gates that reads in part: "I magnif-icently adorned them with luxurious grandeur for all mankind to behold in awe." It seems that imperialism has learned no new tricks in the intervening 2500 years, with the only twist being that the Babylonians are now the object of "behold in awe" from outside rather than from within. Babylon is the legend of the fallen city of grandeur that haunts and inspires modernity at once. Babylon, in this view, is that part of the ancient that is insistently present in the modern but refuses to be accommodated into the usual binary distinctions, like past and present. Let's call this in-between time Babylonian modernity, for short. So now I find myself imag-ining a complex identification with historic and legendary Babylon (not that of Saddam Hussein) and a disidentification with the Babylon of the West. Negotiating Babylon now calls for an ethical, decentered politics and poetics of everyday life in which the visual is as good a means to think as any other, without claiming to tower over other media, or adopting a false modesty in fallen times.

Thinking through Babylon as a metaphor and as a location might enable certain modes of theoretical practice that often seem radi-cally different to work together. That is to say, the epistemic and discursive practices analyzed by the philosopher Michel Foucault seem to hinge around certain profound shifts such as the change between 1750 and 1830 from the public practice of spectacular punishment by torture to the disciplinary prison in which corporal punishment was reduced and conducted out of sight. Edward Said acknowledged Foucault's influence in forming his notion of Orientalism, a (Western) binary distinction between the West and its presumed Others in the mythical "Orient," formed from an imaginary fusion of the Middle East, North Africa and indeed any part of the world with the requisite degree of exoticism from the European point of view. However, Orientalism can at times seem to be a relatively unchanging aspect of Western thought from the late Middle Ages to the present. Unsettling all such binary distinc-tions is Jacques Derrida's theory of *différance* that he understands as being intrinsic to all Western metaphysics. By *différance*, Derrida refers to that which is in difference and deferral at once, terms that are expressed by the same verb *différer* in French. By changing the participle *différence* into the neologism *différance*, Derrida means to suggest that meaning oscillates between difference and its postponement or deferral. In Stuart Hall's view, this is to suggest that "without relations of difference, no representation could occur. But what is then constituted within representation is always open to being deferred, staggered, serialized."[7] One can think of "Babylon" as that part of the "West" that forms a serial mode for the representation of difference that is always deferred. Babylon is, as Derrida writes, the original complication of Western religion and a key player in ancient history. It has been a component of Orientalism in all times but it was rediscovered by Western archaeology in the resonant year 1789, the beginning of the French Revolution. Babylon was in this sense also a product of modern industrial society. In short, medium and long-term views, Babylon is, then, a frame within which differing methodologies and histories can be productively thought alongside each other to generate knowledges that might be in that way different to the received, disciplinary information that surrounds us. I suggest that it offers an epistemology of the visual. That is to say, what we can learn from this intersection of pasts, present and future is the current status of visual knowledge and its possibilities. What results is then a politics, rather than a universal theorization, like the master-slave dialectic. To get to that point, I need to outline how Babylon is to be watched in more detail.

Watching Babylon

As Edward Said writes, reflecting on the twenty-fifth anniversary of his classic publication *Orientalism*, on which the present work is very much dependent:

> Perhaps you will say that I am making too many abrupt transitions between humanistic interpretation on the one hand and foreign policy on the other, and that a modern technological

society, which along with unprecedented power possesses the
Internet and F-16 fighter jets, must in the end be commanded
by formidable technical policy experts, like Donald Rumsfeld
and Richard Perle. But what has really been lost is a sense of the
density and interdependence of human life, which can neither
be reduced to a formula nor brushed aside as irrelevant.[8]

I take that to mean that the renewed emphasis on disciplinarity
and formal skills in the academy leads us to forget what the goal
of our scholarship properly is. At the same time, it points to the
argument of Hardt and Negri that there is no available "outside" in
the present moment of globalization.[9] Every locality is also a part
of the global. Yet, as *Orientalism* reminds us, all localities are by no
means equal. Your view of Babylon depends very much on the
media you might have been able or willing to watch, which are no
longer limited by national boundaries. Rather than provide some
lofty and probably unattainable overview of the war, my goal is to
provoke debate and discussion on the intersected place of the
viewer and the image in the visual event. Image seems an inade-
quate word to deal with the density of the visual in the state of
exception. I have therefore adopted Foucault's concept of the
event. The event is the effect of a network in which subjects operate and which in turn conditions their freedom of action. What
took place in the gym during the American attack on Baghdad was
a small example, and September 11 was the apogee of all such
events. But as Foucault argued, "the problem is at once to distinguish among events, to differentiate the networks and levels to
which they belong, and to reconstitute the lines along which they
are connected and engender one another."[10] He further suggested
that the study of events "works by constructing around the singu-
lar event, analyzed as process, a 'polygon' or, rather, 'polyhedron'
of intelligibility, the number of whose faces is not given in advance
and never properly be taken as finite" (227). That is to say, any
given event can be approached from a potentially infinite number
of viewpoints and must be framed within a series to be intelligible,
as I am doing here by watching the war from Babylon.

There are, one might say, three intersected layers to be prised apart in visual events, as if one were working backwards in a digital imaging program like Adobe Photoshop. These are the locality of the viewer, the contents and contexts of the image, and the global imaginary within which the viewer attempts to makes sense of the screen-images. In this book, each layer is considered in its own section, beginning with my Long Island location as a means of thinking about the circulation anxiety of the American suburbs to which the pictures of the war were most crucially addressed. This viewing location has intense peculiarities that are rarely reflected in external critiques of America. While such critique is certainly politically justified, the hegemonic American dreamworld of Sports Utility Vehicles, superstores and hyperhouses is not the suburbs of *Dallas*, *American Beauty* (1999) or *The Ice Storm* (1997), still less that of the novels of Philip Roth or John Updike. Unlike in Vietnam, extensive coverage of the war in Iraq sustained the level of public consent in the United States, despite vociferous mass opposition. During the invasion of Iraq from March to May 2003, it seems likely that there were more images produced – whether on television, as photography or on the Internet – than in any other comparable period of history. There is a need to engage in some extended visual thinking about what all that watching meant.

Following the precedent of feminist media studies, I mean by watching all the things we do when we watch television: looking, not looking, listening, not listening, eating, making a phone call, working, doing laundry, child care, reading and so on. In short this is a vernacular watching, taking everyday life as its domain. While everyday life has been the focus for feminist and cultural studies for decades, I will suggest that the Iraq war marked a specific moment in the consolidation of globalization as entailing the greatest possible freedom of movement for capital, while restricting the movement of individuals to the circulation of domestic consumption. The resulting circulation anxiety has created a new form of visual subjectivity. Understanding this sensibility will entail a politics and poetics of implication and intersection, moving beyond single media analysis to map a vernacular watching. I borrow the term vernacular from recent calls for studies of vernacular photography, meaning photographs taken by ordinary people and used in everyday situations. If this project has certainly been ventured before – for example, in Situationism, feminist film studies and soap opera analysis – it now needs to be rethought in the context of a digital and global culture of hegemonic capitalism. Watching needs to be thought of as an activity that is necessarily intersected and implicates both other forms of watching and other activities altogether. Watching is a less structured mode of analysis than gaze theory but it has the advantage of being more grounded. At the same time, that watching is haunted by its ancient (and not so ancient) pasts that refuse to simply go to ground. In the Pergamon Museum, there is a Babylonian bowl dating from 2000 BCE. The Hebrew lettering around the inside of the bowl spells out the *Shema Yisroel* (Hear, O Israel), one of the fundamental tenets of Judaism. The bowl is guarded against evil spirits by an anthropomorphic figure drawn on the bottom in a startlingly free fashion, compared with the hierarchic formalities of Assyro-Babylonian art of the period. Vernacular watching is at least as old as this bowl.

Section 1 of this book ("Babylon, Long Island") is devoted to analyzing the mass of television, video, photographic and film images of the war as constituting a network of events. It is not my intent to unmask these images for their deceitful intent, as is so ritualistically done in each case of international conflict in the age of mass media, but to think about the ways in which images have become weapons in the military-visual complex. The opacity of the image in war refused a response: it was a smart weapon in its own right. War images seem to be, like the stealth bombers, hard, sharp-edged and opaque, designed to evade all forms of radar, physical and cultural. Their immunity to criticism is in part a function of their sheer proliferation, especially in times of political crisis. As the media abandon the goal of broadcasting for ever more specific forms of narrow-casting – a pitch to a specific group with shared beliefs, identity or interests – there is always another image available. At the same time, audiences have become both aware of the possibility of manipulating images by technical means and of the wide range of possible interpretations of any given image. The result is a banality of images, to borrow a phrase from philosopher Hannah Arendt, in which the very awareness of the input of the viewer in creating meaning has paradoxically weakened that response. For if all meanings are personal response, the argument goes, then no one meaning has higher priority. It is however important to stress that this banality of images is no accident, but the result of a deliberate effort by those fighting the war to reduce its visual impact by saturating our senses with non-stop indistinguishable and undistinguished images. This policy has had the unintended consequence of making it very hard to create an image of victory. Even the video of the captured Saddam Hussein being subjected to the biopower of America in his medical examination seemed to fade from the memory very quickly. Benjamin responded to the crisis of meaning produced by an excess of information in the First World War by turning to the epic, a form of interactive story-telling that involved "hand, eye, and soul." One present location of such interactivity that has become increasingly significant in recent years is the graphic novel and I contrast examples from the United States, Iran and Israel as means of what Benjamin called preparing to survive civilization.

In Section 3 ("The empire of camps"), I then locate this practice of watching within a new model of globalized power in action. Rather than being based on the disciplinary model of the prison, or the open-ended possibilities of a networked society, the new empire of camps, as I call it, takes the camp for refugees or migrants as its preferred model of social organization. The empire of camps makes its others invisible in a closed-circuit society, seeking to create a reactionary mode of global power in which capital is entirely without restraints but the global workforce is vigorously policed by a detain-and-deport national government. Critic Susan Buck-Morss rightly claims these kinds of interconnections demand the formation of a "global public sphere."[11] Our access to that global public comes from local situated viewing points like Babylon, Long Island, via the non-stop stream of images generated by globalization. Attempts to constitute such a global public should not therefore begin by rejecting questions of difference in favor of a renewed universal.[12] Whatever globalization presently is, it is certainly an imaginary community fissured, like all communities, by gender, sexual and ethnic difference that cannot be wished away. But that is not to call for a simple return to the politics of identity, which have been found wanting in the present crisis. What Said used to call humanism, I will consider as ethics and the relationship to the other, the "ethics of hospitality,"[13] not in the abstract but as applied to a refugee, an asylum seeker or a prisoner. This practice extends and develops the cosmopolitanism of the Enlightenment with reference to the past of the Talmudic tradition, the present crisis and the hope for an ethical future. If there is a certain universality to this concept, it is always encountered and enacted in specific circumstances that inevitably put difference into play.

The visual subject

So let's return to my inability to address the exercise soldier. At the moment of viewing, neither of us really knew what we were seeing, or what its consequences might be. At the same time, this failure of address recalls the now hegemonic theory of the "interpellation" of the subject, developed by the French philosopher Louis Althusser in the 1960s. Althusser described interpellation, or hailing, as something "which can be imagined along the lines of the most commonplace everyday police (or other) hailing 'Hey, you there!'"[14] When we respond to that call by looking round or asking "Do you mean me?" we recognize our interpellation. Derived from Hegel's theory of the dialectic, Althusser's theory of ideology was designed to help us understand how subjects are produced and reproduced. This recognition is the means by which an individual locates itself in time and space. Yet inherent in that little moment is also a visual surveillance that leads to a sense of detection or recognition. The actions of the subject are suspicious but their actions clearly exist. Rather than an exchange between individuals on foot, as presumed in Althusser's theory of inter-pellation, his former colleague Jacques Rancière has recently argued that the modern anti-spectacle now dictates that there is nothing to see and that instead one must keep moving, keep cir-culating and keep consuming: "The police are above all a certitude about what is there, or rather, about what is not there: 'Move along, there's nothing to see.'"[15] The police interpellate us not as individuals but as part of traffic, which must move on by that which is not to be seen. One of the new camps for migrants or refugees concealed in a remote area of the countryside is a good example of this object of visuality, which is there and not there at once.

Here we find ourselves at that crux of time, space and visuality which is at the heart of this project. For, as Rancière continues:

> The police say there is nothing to see, nothing happening, nothing to be done, but to keep moving, circulating; they say that the space of circulation is nothing but the space of circu-lation. Politics consists in transforming that space of circulation into the space of the manifestation of a subject: be it the people, workers, citizens. It consists in reconfiguring that space, what there is to do there, what there is to see or name. It is a dispute about the division of what is perceptible to the senses.

That is to say, it is an epistemology of the subject, defined by its knowledge rather than its Being. Insofar as that dispute concerns the visual, necessarily interfaced with the other senses, this politics of bringing the subject into presence in space is visual culture. Placing the visual subject in the zone of circulation described by Rancière suggests that the contemporary visual subject is not quite Benjamin's nineteenth-century flâneur, or dandy, observing while unobserved. And while visual agency might interestingly be explored by psychoanalysis, this is not a properly psychoanalytic gaze theory because it deals with individuals in relation to specific discursive practices. On the other side of the equation, while Foucault's theory of panopticism clearly deals with people as the object of visuality, my revision of his vital work (see Section 3) allows a measure of visual agency to the visual subject, although that possibility is a form of "weak" power, to use Michel de Certeau's distinction. The opponent of the war, like myself, watching the non-stop stream of images from Iraq is a good example of the visual subject, a person all but overwhelmed by visual materials that they cannot control but cannot refuse to watch. For when the police say there is nothing to see, they are not telling the truth; nor are we supposed to infer that they are. Rather they mean, "while there is something to see, you have no authority or need to look at it." By being simply a citizen, one does not necessarily attain the full authority of the visual subject, the person who is allowed and required to look in all circumstances.

There is a noticeable global divide according to degrees of visual subjectivity that requires its own activism and engagement. To even be able to watch, as I watched the exercise soldier watching, implies a certain position within the hierarchies of globalization that can in one way be measured by relationships to visual media. The global population is divided into roughly two halves, one of which has access to television in some way and one that does not. Needless to say the section that is not watching television is quite closely matched with that half of the world population that has yet to make a telephone call, exists on three dollars a day or less, and does not have regular access to clean drinking water. The television-watching group is by no means homogeneous. Someone watching al-Jazeera is going to have had a very different experience of the war in Iraq than the habitué of Rupert Murdoch's Fox News. This group can further be arranged into three sectors according to their overall wealth and power. Within it are the 500 million people with access to the Internet, the global middle class. A somewhat smaller but hard to quantify sector is constituted by those people making and using digital or moving image themselves, using camcorders and digital cameras. Analog cameras are now relegated to the back of American technology stores, although they are still the basic democratic tool of visual imagery on a global basis. Dominating the visual sector of globalization are a very small number of people and corporations who own the visual means of production, such as Rupert Murdoch's News Corporation, the ABC/Disney empire, Microsoft and AOL TimeWarner. With such former heavyweights as Ted Turner having been eliminated from this elite sector, it can safely be said that for all the proliferation of visual images, films and television programming, the ownership of these media is more concentrated than it has ever been.

But not so fast.[16] To think of watching the war against Iraq in only these terms would be to think from the point of view of the police. Seen from the ground in Baghdad, the "shock and awe" campaign was no shock, and whatever awe was inspired dissipated quickly. Even after the end of the first Gulf War in 1991, there had been almost constant warfare in the "no-fly" zones created in northern and southern Iraq, while the economic blockade had caused great hardship. As the fighting progressed and it became clear that initial claims to have eliminated the Iraqi leadership were exaggerated, the Western audience also became adjusted to the sight of explosions. As I write with the war officially over but with more Iraqi and Occupation casualties by the day, and with the search for weapons of mass destruction thoroughly discredited, it's hard to feel awe. Instead of moral and visual clarity, all is confusion. The most striking example of this visual revisionism has come in the new version of the carefully choreographed announcement by President George W. Bush of the end of major hostilities on May 1, 2003. Standing on the USS *Abraham Lincoln*, the president spoke under a large banner reading "Mission Accomplished." However, by late October the number of American personnel killed in action after the declared end of the war had come to exceed those lost during the official war period. At this point, the president disavowed his own banner, claiming that it was created at the instigation of the aircraft carrier's crew. In this short space of time, one of the most striking visual images of the war has now come to convey at least two very different meanings, even within the American pro-war audience. In order to place another image in the public attention, Bush flew to Baghdad at Thanksgiving to celebrate the holiday with the American troops, during which time he presented them with a turkey. The inevitable photograph was seen across the United States. It later emerged that this turkey was a fake, created by the military kitchen staff to generate a sense of holiday atmosphere. By now, one began to sense that faking it was in fact official policy, as Naomi Klein has argued: "This was the year [2003] when fakeness ruled: fake rationales for war, a fake President dressed as a fake soldier declaring a fake end to combat and then holding up a fake turkey."[17] In short, any attempt to think critically about watching the war will have to roam much further than the official images of war and their counterparts in the alternative media if it is to produce anything more than the visual equivalent of an echo.

Babylonian modernity II

So this book is the product of an interplay between the dream image of Babylon and the visual subject in the current emergency. This dynamic is given urgency by the important, if constantly unsettling, place of Babylon in and as the visual image of modernity that contains and evokes the ancient past. The complexities of space and time experienced in modern visuality that generate the image of Babylon do so in a conscious and unconscious echo of ancient traditions. At the same time, modernity's visual character has consistently seemed to recall Babylon since the beginnings of industrial capitalism. The nineteenth-century American writer Ralph Waldo Emerson was struck by the new style adopted by his friend Thomas Carlyle in the latter's history of the French Revolution. Writing in 1837, Emerson told Carlyle: "I think you see in pictures." Musing on the effect, he added that "it has the aroma of Babylon," by which he meant the complexity of the modern metropolis.[18] Modernity, as epitomized by the French Revolution, was in this view at once visualized and Babylonian.

One man who linked the two realms of urban culture was William Henry Fox Talbot, the British inventor of photography. Talbot became sufficiently expert in cuneiform writing that he was the adjudicator of a debate over the deciphering of the ancient language for the Royal Academy in 1857.[19] Emerson's sense that the world-picture of modernity was Babylonian can be traced throughout modern Western art history from William Blake's prophetic evocations of the *Whore of Babylon* to Edgar Degas' early fascination with the Babylonian queen Semiramis (1861) and the popular nineteenth-century genre of Orientalist painting that was filled with images of Babylon. One central example is the British artist Edwin Long's notorious painting *The Babylonian Marriage Market* (1875), at that time the most expensive painting ever sold. Long's painting depicted a slave market for women, with one woman being unveiled on the block as the others wait for their turn. The conceit of the piece depends on the invisibility of the unrobed woman whose back faces the viewer. Her beauty has to be judged from the pleased reactions of the watching Babylonian men. The anthropological visualization continued with the row of waiting women, who formed a racialized color scale, from the "low" point of a dark skin, via the Asian, to the "high" of the white woman. This mix of race, gender and sexuality in a historicized frame was perhaps the perfect expression of high Victorian establishment sensibility.

This fascination was given life by the invention of Assyria, Babylon and Mesopotamia in the archaeology of the nineteenth century, during which the historical sites of Nineveh and Babylon were first excavated (see Section 3).[20] These discoveries were themselves influenced by the depiction of Babylon in Western art, such as the monumental canvases of the British artist John Martin and his *Fall of Babylon* (1819). This painting was so realistic in its perspectival effects that a barrier had to be placed in front of it to stop people from trying to walk into it. The painting served as the archetype both for the architectural reconstruction of the site itself and its depiction in even quite recent historical accounts. Its intense realism was adopted for the mise-en-scène of the classic silent film *Intolerance* (1916), directed by D.W. Griffith.[21] The Babylonian sense of modernity that Martin had visualized thus influenced the material remains of Assyro-Babylonian culture, the definitive modern medium of cinema and the historical representation of Babylon. Griffith also used Long's *Babylonian Marriage Market* to create the mise-en-scène for the attempted sale of his heroine The Mountain Girl, a character whose rural innocence and fortitude contrasts strongly with the decadent Babylonians. She is rescued from the block by the intervention of Belshazzar, who gives her a cuneiform tablet indicating her freedom. In turn, the scenes of Babylonian decadence in *Intolerance* have become a cinematic archetype, evoked most recently in *The Matrix Reloaded* (2003), when the rebel city Zion has a rave in defiance of the approaching war machines. This image makes sense because Zion is not Israel but the site of exile from the devastated "real world" dominated by the machines. In this insistent interplay of "image" and "reality," Babylon is persistently recreated as a visual event that is neither simply fictitious nor wholly real in the common-sense meaning of the term but evokes the fractured and layered sense of the experience of modernity.

It is in this sense that Babylon has also played an important role in religion and other theories of anti-modernity. It has been a powerful figure in modern Christianity, whose spectre has haunted modernity just as much as that of communism. In the writer Edmund Gosse's memoir of growing up in evangelical Victorian England, his own sense of scientific rationality was strongly contrasted with the evangelical beliefs of his parents who were members of the Plymouth Brethren. The one amusement his parents permitted themselves was to read the Book of Revelations as a history of the then present. Gosse recalled how, aided by popular published guides to the text,

> They were helped by these guides to recognise in wild Oriental visions direct statements regarding Napoleon III and Pope Pius IX and the King of Piedmont, historic figures which they conceived of as foreshadowed, in language which admitted of plain interpretation, under the names of denizens of Babylon and companions of the Wild Beast.[22]

This sense that the wilder passages of the Bible predicted the upheavals of modernity and the triumph of the elect has dominated American evangelical Christianity in the past thirty years. During the war in Iraq, Tim LaHaye, a self-proclaimed scholar of Biblical prophecy, published *Babylon Rising*, the latest in his series of Christian novels that have sold over 50 million copies. *Babylon Rising* is a new departure for LaHaye, written in conjunction with Greg Dinallo, a secular thriller writer. It tells the story of Michael Murphy, a Christian (male) Lara Croft, whose expert knowledge of Biblical archaeology leads him into a conflict with the evil Talon over a magical figure created at the time of Nebuchadnezzar in Babylon. Its evangelical, eschatological view of history is radically different from that of the secular mainstream. It is shared by Christian historians like Forrest Watson and James Draper, who write on US history from an evangelical perspective:

> For a historian who does not believe in God, the facts in this [book] will have been put together in a most unscientific manner. But if you accept the fact of a God who controls history, the conclusion is obvious. The providence of God was at work.[23]

It is this sense of divinely determined history that guided the second invasion of Iraq, signalled to the faithful by George W. Bush when he cited the anti-Babylonian prophet Isaiah in his notorious victory speech of May 1, 2003. In Isaiah, we read that "Babylon, the glory of kingdoms, the beauty of the Chaldee's excellency, shall be as when God overthrew Sodom and Gomorrah . . . her time is near to come and her days shall not be prolonged" (Isaiah, Chapter 13, verse 19). This association of Babylon with the legendary deviants of Sodom is a resonance that echoes through the recent war (see Section 3, "The empire of camps"). Even those working in the secular media adopted this prophetic approach. CNN journalist Sandra Mackey opined in a short account of Saddam Hussein's career that:

the kings of Assyria never accepted the reality that empires, like modern states, survive only through a measure of consent by the governed. Like a series of ancient Saddam Husseins, each failed to lay the basis of a durable state.[24]

The implication of the passage is that the rulers of the region have been and remain terminally incapable of creating an effective nation state, due to their inability to achieve "consent," thus requiring the assistance of outsiders.

Babylon as an image of exile has also been a metaphor for the site of resistance and recuperation. To support his argument that it was in America that the Irish had learned "what indomitable forces nationality possesses," the playwright, novelist and wit Oscar Wilde put Irishness in play both with Jewish and African diasporas, the former directly, the latter by implication. In a review of W.B. Yeats' collection of Irish fairy tales, Wilde opined in 1889 that "what captivity was to the Jews, exile has been to the Irish."[25] This comparison was more often made between African exile in the Americas than with the Irish so Wilde achieved a measure of surprise with his figure, while continuing his fascination with reading the modern as a return of the ancient. The currency of the metaphor of Jewish exile was attested in a pamphlet written in Sierra Leone for publication in Liverpool in 1898 by the pan-Africanist Edward Wilmot Blyden, who again posed the relationship as an analogy: "The Hebrews could not see or serve God in the land of the Egyptians; no more can the Negro under the Anglo-Saxon." While preferring to cite the Egyptian captivity rather than the Babylonian exile, Blyden asserted that his metaphor indicated that Africans should return to Africa. Furthermore, as both Liberia's sometime ambassador to Britain, and a former British official in her West African colonies, he declared: "Africa appeals to the Jew . . . to come with his scientific and other culture, gathered by his exile in many lands, and with his special spiritual endowments, to the assistance of Africa."[26] Blyden's text was not, then, simply a metaphor. He expressed the experience of African and Jewish passage as directly comparable in their need

for emancipation and their experience of exile, couched in religious terms. At precisely this time the British government was
actively considering resettling the Jews in Uganda, a proposal that
was endorsed by the founder of Zionism, Theodore Herzl, in
1903. Nonetheless, it was rejected at the Seventh Zionist Congress
of 1905, causing a split in the Zionist movement. As postcolonial
theorist Dipesh Chakrabarty argues, such literal and metaphorical translations "appeal to models of cross-cultural and cross-
categorical translations that do not take a universal middle term
for granted."[27] In this case, it would mean that Africans and Jews
imagined themselves as translatable figures of Babylonian exile that
did not need to be mediated through the white colonizer.

Consequently, Babylon is a key image in the syncretic religion
Rastafari that developed in Jamaica during the 1930s and 40s and
now has influence throughout the African diaspora. Rastafari
appropriated symbols and legends from the Old Testament into
its message of a return to Africa and African empowerment that
was embodied by the monarchy of Haile Selassie in Ethiopia
(1892–1975), which gave substance to the idea of a black sovereign. Rastafari uses Babylon as a figure for Western capitalism,
derived from the Jewish exile in Babylon. With their 1971 hit "By
the Rivers of Babylon" and its subsequent cover versions, the
reggae band The Melodians exported this intersected metaphor
from Jamaican Rastafari culture to the contemporary Western
world. Again, the comparisons are not exact but implied and intersected. The street disturbances and riots in Notting Hill, Brixton,
Toxteth and other black neighborhoods in British cities from 1976
to 1983 were what Max Romeo in a hit song of the period called
"War in Babylon" (1976). The idea was adopted by many punk
bands, like The Ruts with their independent hit "Babylon's
Burning" (1978). As I grew up in London at this time, it's striking
to recall how segregated British society was at a time when the
appalling *Black and White Minstrel Show*, an unabashed blackface
minstrel show of the Dixie kind, was still on BBC television as
primetime entertainment. Paul Gilroy has described the Rastafarian movement in Britain of the 1970s as a mixed formation in

which "overt resistance is tied to strategic negotiation and other more subtle and refined forms of political antagonism."[28] In this sense, "Babylon" was at once the police, capitalism, colonialism, slavery, anti-cannabis laws and so on. To this extent, "Babylon" was a significant means of expressing and contesting a relationship to economic and political power in everyday life. This layered sense of culture was made palpable in the sound systems of the period. A hit like "War in Babylon" would be played at appropriately "trouser shaking" volume – loud enough that your trousers shook against your leg – engineered in such a way that the vocals seemed to float high above the fundamentals of the rhythm, drums and bass that interplayed at your feet. You could literally dance on the sound.

What do we make of these interstices, implications and intersections? Not that the legend and history of Babylon in some sense caused the war or can neatly explain it. But this recurring sense of apocalypse in Babylon expresses the eternal return that Benjamin, himself following Nietzsche, highlighted as modernity's spectre. The politics and poetics of implication, intersection and interstices that are my subject here offer no exit from the labyrinth. My project is to refuse the designation of a neatly divided world where peoples and nations are offered stark choices to be with "us" or against "us," whether that we is the United States, al-Qa'ida, or the Taliban. Modernity's network cannot be reverse-engineered into a feudal hierarchy, despite the global reaction against the emergent "network society" of the 1990s.[29] As Foucault emphasized, power always creates resistance. So the goal is not to find the place of resistance, for that necessarily exists already. A resistance that succeeds simply becomes power. Borrowing Benjamin's sense of utopia, I suggest at the end of each section one means in which a way of living without the police might be imagined. Such utopian imagining is a necessary cultural response to the gloom-laden chorus that there is no alternative to the current doctrine of pre-emptive war and the politics of fear. It pays homage to Edward Said's belief that a university ought to be a utopian space, without losing sight for an instant of the politics of knowledge.

One name for such a politics opposed to the all-encompassing ambitions of the police might be anarchism. It is the anarchy of the dream world and dream image, rather than actually existing anarchic politics. In this regard, I imply by anarchism what Walter Benjamin meant by "messianism": the chance to imagine that the world might suddenly become a strikingly different and better place. But, as he liked to recall, it was said in the Talmud that the messiah would come and make one small but vital change. Consequently, his friend Gerschom Scholem described their youthful position as "theocratic anarchism."[30] Something of that tension between the universal and the local, so relevant to today's crises, survived into Benjamin's contradictory and dynamic version of Marxism. It might be said that sustaining these contradictions in dialogue is the difference of anarchism. It is that which allowed the American Jewish feminist Emma Goldman to cite Oscar Wilde's theory of the necessity of freedom to choose one's work in her classic 1917 essay on anarchism.[31] It later enabled Constant, the Dutch Situationist, to imagine his utopian society as New Babylon. What time is the time of this contradictory dream image that I am calling Babylonian modernity? It is not the time of the "end," whether of history, the human, or that of the "post," as in post-colonial, or post-structuralism. Nor is this the future perfect of the spectre in which all issues will have been resolved and all ghosts finally laid to rest.[32] This is a time that looks to the future but with a sense of a transient present haunted by the past. It is twilight. In this "twilight of the digerati"[33] that is also a twilight of capitalism, it is too early to see Minerva's owls flying: we must wait for a dusk that is eternally postponed. In the failing light, we need to find our way around a network in which the links are broken, the sites not maintained, the fiber dark and the power out. Don't be afraid: they have no idea where you want to go today.

Section 1: Babylon, Long Island

Watching war, an activity to which we have become accustomed since the rise of global television, is a curious phenomenon. Of all viewing experiences, it is the most intensely "live," in that it exists to witness the extinction of human life. Yet, like soldiering itself, it is for the most part an exercise in tedium. The 2003 war in Iraq raised the experience to new heights, saturating channels that only a few years previously had covered the stock market with similar non-stop enthusiasm. The constant updates, announcements of breaking news, switches to live press announcements and the circulation around the various correspondents and fixed cameras available reinforced a sense that this watching was present tense only. The strategy of "embedding" reporters with military units provided a means of identification for the American television viewer with the live images, even when there was very little to see. In contesting this visual narrative, it is necessary to begin by refusing this apparently transparent link to the remote site of warfare. Such images are legible for US audiences by virtue of the traditional film and television format in which an opening panoramic shot of a city skyline establishes the general location, followed by a gradual zoom in by the camera to reveal the star or hero of the piece. Such careful geographical locating of the viewer is now accomplished by the popular jump cut – an edit that "jumps" from one location to the next – a function that is compressed into the "live" news link. All this spatial and temporal jumping creates an idealized "American" viewpoint that has no specificity. So this section takes its time by refusing to jump into the image until a place from which to watch the war has been identified.

The place of watching has become elusive because, as we saw in the Prologue, modern anti-spectacle dictates that there is in fact nothing to see and that instead one must keep moving, keep circulating and keep consuming. Jacques Rancière's interaction of politics and space recalls Donna Haraway's feminist theory of located viewing that she called "situated knowledges."[1] So what I want to attempt here is a situated critique from the no-place of the modern suburb that integrates both Rancière's theory of the subject and Haraway's feminist politics. For when critics have responded to Haraway's call, they have tended to locate themselves in subcultural urban environments. The suburbs are regarded with distaste as the domain of "placelessness" that threatens to encroach on the situated urban environment. However, most Americans no longer live in cities and the politics of subcultures have become very well understood by consumer capitalism. The hegemonic residential environment is now the suburbs, that extensive and wide-ranging combination of housing, extensive service industries, health and education facilities made possible by high property prices and low-wage manual and service labor. Let's acknowledge at once that this is a contestation of America from within, and that other very different accounts have and will be written from other places. But it seems to me important to look at the American suburb because of its extraordinary peculiarity and specificity that is predicated by American mass culture as "normality." From this "normal" viewpoint, others can be seen as "pathological," as in George W. Bush's repeated assertion that Saddam Hussein is a "madman." While reports and media from overseas are part of American everyday life, as I shall show, I cannot recreate the situated experience of watching the war in London, Delhi or Tokyo. Arundhati Roy has written about the war from India, John Docker has written from Australia, Tariq Ali from Britain and so on. Globalization creates a second "birth of the reader," to appropriate Roland Barthes' old phrase, in that it is the reader/viewer of these differing and disparate texts and images who occupies the position of judgment.

The American suburbs will not stand revealed at the end of this analysis as the locale of a hitherto unexpected resistance to global capitalism. After all, this is not a subculture so much as it is the majority version of American everyday life. It is the enactment of Rancière's vision of contemporary space as being the space of circulation, where there is nothing to see. In the shopping and commuter-oriented suburbs, circulation is all. The question is, as Rancière suggests, whether this space of circulation can also be made the space for the emergence of a political and visual subject. To do so, we will have to understand the circulation anxiety of (sub)urban life. The modern suburb is not simply an absence – whether of culture, subculture or intelligence – but an intersection of signs that implicate others, in very much the way that is usually associated with urban life. That "poetics of implication," as Robert Blair St. George has called it, that texture of suburban living, is as old as white settlement, which is to say, not very old. St. George, a folklorist working on early New England, argues that: "Poetics of implication introduces a loose, open-ended structure of feeling that works through indirection and intertextuality to create a dynamic center for political play."[2] Although St. George was writing about colonial culture, his interaction of Raymond Williams' structure of feeling, with poststructuralist analysis, and the richly intersected notion of *homo ludens* – the person who plays – applies very well to our newly colonial suburbia. I would add to his poetics a politics that aspire to be at once personal, local and global in the manner suggested by Haraway. What the Situationists once called "the colonization of everyday life" entails this politics and poetics of implication and intersection. St. George argues that the poetics of implication can be effectively traced through performance and place, both of course key terms in cultural studies. My intention is to supplement that work by bringing it to bear on the unfamiliar territory of the American suburb and by considering the exigencies of the present as newly distinct from the postmodern moment in which feminism and cultural studies developed these ideas.

In the case of visual culture, the poetics of implication are one fruitful means of approaching what I will call vernacular watching.[3] Based on work in feminist media studies and cultural studies, vernacular watching refers to the divergent and diverse act of looking in everyday life by which individuals become situated as visual subjects. Watching, as I mentioned earlier on, is the wide variety of things we do and places we are when we watch television. At the same time, vernacular watching tends to emphasize those moments of drift in which the attention is not fully engaged in gazing at visual media. To this end, it is intrigued by channel surfing rather than appointment television, web-surfing at work, or, to borrow a term from Anna McCarthy, the encounter with ambient media (media out of their "proper" place, such as art outside the gallery or television outside the home).[4] Vernacular watching is perhaps epitomized by the looking that is done while waiting, whether in a formal waiting room, in a car, or for some appointment. Waiting engenders boredom and distraction, the marks of a certain counter to modernity as Walter Benjamin has described them. Consequently, vernacular watching takes place in the corner of one's eye, the passing detail that catches a glance or the sideways look at a fellow waiter. This is the transient and trans-dimensional way of seeing that visual culture seeks to define, describe and deconstruct as the transverse look or glance. The transverse glance is not a gaze because it resists the imperial domain of gendered sexuality, using what Judith Halberstam has called "the transgender gaze."[5] If this seems a little utopian, let it also be said that this transverse practice is at all times at risk of being undercut by transnational capital.

The vernacular glance sideways has several components. It is the glance that we use to look at the incident which the police urge us to move on past because there is nothing to see. It has in it that averted viewing used by astronomers to detect low-light objects by avoiding the central cones of the eye. Cultural averted viewing is done so as to better detect the faint emissions of that which is hard to see in the glare of the contemporary spectacle. Averted vision does not direct the gaze at an object but it does direct the attention. In this way, a vernacular glance sideways is a conscious effort of perceptual manipulation as well as the chance encounter in the corner of one's eye. There are two consequences of this manipulated attention. First, it makes the watcher highly conscious of the act of watching, open to the fear of detection. Second, by diverting attention away from what is apparently in front of the viewer, it challenges the "attention economy" in which value is created by attracting our attention.[6] It is with this peripheral vision that one both maintains a covert look at someone or something and becomes aware that one is being looked at, whether with desire, sexual or racial surveillance, or by another bored person waiting. It is therefore inherently complicated rather than being a simple "progressive" response to reactionary societal surveillance as manifested by the closed-circuit television camera (see Section 3). It has elements of what the African American artist Kara Walker calls the "sidelong glance." Walker's sidelong glance evokes the content of her dramatic cut-outs that depict the violent, bodily, and sexual dimensions to slavery that exist in the margins of the religiously inflected slave narratives. She herself asserts that this art is designed to provoke a different kind of viewing from her audience: "I really wanted to find a way to make work that could lure viewers out of themselves and into this fantasy."[7] At the same time, the sidelong glance recalls the averted glance of the subaltern, the enslaved and the colonized in historical experience. So rather than separate ways of seeing into media-specific theories of spectatorship, whether for art, film, or television, I want to consider watching as the multi-media site-specific performance of everyday life. Here I am adapting St. George's vocabulary of performance and place to that of avant-garde art in the manner of the Situationists in order to suggest that there is no unmediated visual interface with the world.

What is seen becomes interesting when it is seen at a particular time in a given place. Cultural geographers have been working for two decades to shift our understanding of place as being the intersection of physical space with cultural discourse and power. For example, Allen R. Pred, cited by St. George, urges us to think of place as "an appropriation and transformation of space and nature that is inseparable from the reproduction and transformation of society in time and space."[8] The suburb, in this view, radically tries to prevent the formation of place by displacing time and space from modernist concepts of transformation and progress into timeless fantasies of utopia. As such it is the most advanced form of the spatialized politics described by Rancière. As suburbanites keep moving, insistently told that there is nothing to see, only shopping to do, they are describing with these patterns of movement what Marx once called "the soul of the commodity." Time in the suburbs has lost the urgency of progressive modernity and has returned to a medieval sense of the seasons, only here the seasons are replaced by holidays. The year is marked by the transition from one holiday to the next, with decorations and merchandising for the next holiday appearing as soon as one is over. Education at elementary schools follows the same pattern so that autumn leaf projects are followed by Thanksgiving studies of Native Americans. The circuit is given coherence, a end that is also a beginning, by "The Holidays." By this expression is meant the blend of Christmas, Hannukah, Kwanzaa, New Year's Eve and all such other winter solstice events into a mass frenzy of consumption. As The Holidays end the year begins and the suburbs ready themselves for Valentine's Day, only six short weeks away. In this paradise neither lost nor regained but endlessly deferred, there are other implications. In this section, I will consider my own place and sites of watching, and move on to think about what was seen from those locations during the war in the next section. Rather than look to high art, whether as film or the visual arts, for the site of mediating the war, I shall consider vernacular watching in its now hegemonic sites in suburban America: the hyperhouse, the superstore and the Sports Utility Vehicle (SUV).

Suburban Babylon

So to begin with Long Island, New York, where I live and where I watched the war, and where there is a Babylon of our own. The abject other to the metropolis of New York, Long Island has been described by Lou Reed, a native, as the "armpit of the universe." It is Long Island's very lack of appeal to East Village media and cultural sophisticates that makes it interesting as a site of vernacular watching. Long Island is, as the name suggests, a long, thin island adjacent to the island of Manhattan. One hundred and ten miles long and only fourteen miles wide, it is the site of two of the boroughs of New York City, Queens and Brooklyn. Further east are commuter suburbs, ex-urbs that seem to be suburbs but do not move in the orbit of New York; a little remaining farmland, mostly for wine; and the gilded estates of the Hamptons. Long Island is also home to the town of Babylon, incorporated in the late nineteenth century as part of one of the original eight towns on the island created by the British colonists. Settled since the mid-seventeenth century, Babylon took its name from an estate named New Babylon, founded in 1803 by one Nathaniel Conklin, made wealthy by the paper mill established by his father.[9] This unlikely name for Protestant New England arose when Conklin's mother sniffed at his choice of location, calling it "another Babylon." The name has curious echoes, both of the Situationist project New Babylon, and the Orientalist assumption that Baghdad was New Babylon. On Long Island, Babylon was a stop on the stagecoach out of New York City and home to the notorious American Hotel. On June 1, 1843, Isabella van Wagenen decided to leave New York City and change her name to boot. When she arrived in Long Island as Sojourner Truth, she headed for Huntington.[10] Along the way in a curious incident, she was put up for the night by a strange couple who insisted on taking her to a ball, with drinking and dancing to the small hours.[11] This place may not have actually been Babylon – though it must have been close – but for Truth, now committed to the Millerite Evangelicals, it was certainly Babylon in the metaphorical sense. One figure who definitely did visit the new Babylon was Oscar Wilde, who gave a lecture there during his American tour of 1882. It is a matter of debate as to whether his thoughts on "The House Beautiful" properly took root in Long Island's sandy soil.

Figure 1.1 The village of Babylon, Long Island

Despite this history, Long Island is a place that urban sophisticates and decadents have long sought to escape in keeping with
the modern American drama of urban relocation and self-
discovery, epitomized in Jack Kerouac's 1957 book *On the Road*
and in films like *Easy Rider* (1969). For many others, green suburbs
with decent schools and low crime rates form an attractive "bourgeois utopia," to quote the title of the 1989 pioneering study of
suburbs by Robert Fishman. Yet this utopia is thin on the ground,
as countless films, novels and photographs have pointed out. The
difference is now that the city no longer provides an automatic
refuge from suburban anomie. The keynote of contemporary
(white) middle-class life in towns, cities and suburbs is circulation
anxiety, stemming from a worry about what that "nothing to see,"
which Rancière's police keep us away from, really is. Knowing
very well that there is in fact something to see, we move on
nonetheless, worrying about what it was that we couldn't see and
obeying the command out of a general sense of foreboding. The

Figure 1.2 An 1806 house in Babylon

events of 9-11 were, in this sense, the culmination of a long habitation with fear, registered in terms of race and international politics, formerly communism, now terrorism. These motivated anxieties register as alienation, neurosis and above all as the desire to consume. Consumption is here, as befits a settler society, the act of generating (white) social space, a Babylon of the domestic, featuring extravagant Babylonian spaces in oversized cars and oversized houses sheltering oversized TVs. Here I think of the opening sequence of the hit TV series *The Sopranos*. We see Tony, a middle-aged man with a cigar, driving his SUV along the post-industrial wilderness of the New Jersey Turnpike, past the relics of first and second generation immigration like the pork store, the pizza palace and the modest one-family home, to arrive at his hyperhouse, the scene of the internal drama that will then be analyzed by the psychoanalyst Doctor Melfi. To retreat from this world, Tony goes to watch the History Channel on TV, the all-Hitler-all-the-time history-as-entertainment channel. In this televisual retreat, Tony finds watching documentaries about the Second World War to be a place where good and evil are clearly defined and distinguished, literally in black and white, unlike the chaos of his own life. *The Sopranos* rewrites the public sphere as the private world of cars, houses, and family, and makes disfunction into narrative.

SUV vision

So, let's consider the cars. In a place where it is almost impossible to drive off-road because every plot of land is owned by somebody, the vehicle of choice is consistently the Sports Utility Vehicle, which has replaced the station wagon of earlier generations. The reason routinely cited for their popularity is a sense of safety generated by the huge trucks. As SUVs score poorly on safety tests and are notorious for rolling over while turning even at relatively low speeds, the safety being referred to is not one of those much-touted but rarely observed rational market choices. Rather, the high viewpoint provided by these vehicles and their sense of invulnerability reassures the perennially nervous suburban resident that, once inside, nothing can get at them. Whose viewpoint are we discussing here? Early SUVs were marketed directly at men and had suitably butch names like the Isuzu Trooper, and the popular Jeep line of SUVs is in fact derived from Second World War military vehicles. But as more and more women became SUV drivers, these vehicles' names came to take on resonances of the digital frontier, with titles like the Ford Explorer and the Lincoln Navigator directly borrowing the names of the most popular web browsers. Perhaps the only honestly named SUV is the vast Chevy Suburban, which gained credibility as Tony Soprano's vehicle of choice. With their tinted windows and height off the ground, SUVs offer a place from which both men and women can masquerade at riding the American (digital) frontier without risk and without

Figure 1.3 McSUV

being seen watching. That is to say, from within the SUV it is possible to imagine being the police.

This viewpoint might also be equated with the masquerade of masculinity theorized by Laura Mulvey as that of the female spectator in narrative cinema. Of course, Mulvey's mode of film theory rested on the notion of the immobile spectator in the dream state induced by cinema, while the SUV driver is obviously moving. In the modern vehicle, only children newly immobilized in seatbelts and car seats are such spectators, willing or unwilling spectators of in-vehicle television. Advertising for such devices displays the children quietly ignoring mesas in the Utah desert or flowing rivers in a wilderness in favor of *Spongebob Squarepants*, the cult cartoon on Nickelodeon. Only the driver has to engage his or her vision in the ideal SUV. In the gridlocked, traffic-controlled environment of modern America, there is plenty of excess vision to engage, as the countless roadside advertisements and signs suggest. If the pun can be forgiven, in the suburban vehicle one is not so much driving as performing the Situationist *dérive*, a "technique of transient passage through varied ambiences."[12] Further, while Mulvey's theory of the gaze pertained to cinema as an institution, the SUV viewpoint is experienced as a specifically American form of empowered citizenship. Being America, SUV citizenship has taken on a religious tinge. In a poll conducted in July 2003 by the reputable Pew organization, 29 percent of Americans questioned felt that Jesus would drive an SUV. To be fair 30 percent did not think so but only 7 percent suggested he might walk instead. During the second Gulf War, SUVs became directly politicized, as opponents of the war argued that the *casus belli* was to preserve cheap fuel for the gas-guzzling SUV, while hawks came to represent SUVs as the patriotic and even religious choice, and the war itself was fought by soldiers travelling in Humvees. For a number of years the Humvee has been the ultra SUV of choice. In the imagination of the SUV driver, its military background and vast size effectively convey the implication that the owner is to be feared. Realizing the commercial potential of their vehicle, Hummer created a civilian version officially known as the H2. The original H1 sells for around $100,000 but the H2 is about $50,000 basic. Most dealers sell them fully equipped with luxury extras. For example, you can buy a $449 remote control for the Hummer equipped with spy camera. Even at these prices, Hummer sells about 3000 units a month. As a metonym of modern America, the new owners get a tax deduction of $36,000 because their vehicles qualify as trucks.

The Iraq war became in effect an extended commercial for the vehicle. During the invasion, one Hummer owner was quoted in the *New York Times*: "When I turn on the TV, I see wall-to-wall Hummers, and I'm proud." This act of vernacular watching – the casual switching on of a television – comes to be figured as an act of political agency that overwrites the indeterminacy associated with everyday life. The truck itself is now represented by the Hummer Owners Group as a symbol of freedom: "[T]he freedom of choice, the freedom of happiness, the freedom of adventure and

Figure 1.4 Alfredo Juan and Isabel Aquilizan, *Project M201 In God We Trust*, 2003 stainless steel, video, sound and domestic objects 160 × 380 × 180 cm
(Courtesy of the Philippine National Commission for Culture and the Arts; photo by R.J. Fernandez)

discovery, and the ultimate freedom of expression . . . Those who deface a Hummer in words or deed deface the American flag and what it stands for."[13] The Hummer is, it appears, now beyond the reach of the First Amendment, which protects the right to free speech. It comes as no surprise to learn that the celebrity spokesperson for the Hummer Owners Group is Arnold Schwarzenegger, one time body-builder and now governor of California. In late August 2003 the Earth Liberation Front torched a Hummer dealership, accusing the vehicles of being "gas guzzling polluters." The H2 drives eleven miles to the gallon, about average for the vast range, such as the Suburban which does thirteen but only costs $40,000. This symbolic action prompted a retort by the Southern Californian Hummer Owners Group, who staged a drive-by of the dealership with some 20 Hummers and H2s. No need to ask how these people voted in the California election. The symbolism here is more than a clash of environmental politics. It is the deployment of a resurgent and vengeful gender normativity, less interested in sex than power, seeking to end the "gender-bending" of the 1990s. In this view, the "queer eye" that has emerged into vernacular culture via the hit television show *Queer Eye for the Straight Guy*, is itself normative of queer as a series of clichés about interior decoration, fashion and hair, rather than the transgressive politics epitomized by the activism of Queer Nation.

In this sense, blending the philosopher Jurgen Habermas' theory of the bourgeois public sphere and Volvo advertising, one can think of the automotive space as "the bourgeois steel sphere." In Habermas' view, the public sphere depends on "the interiority of the conjugal family." The family provides not just stability and security but is rather the locus of rationality itself:

> The experiences about which a public passionately concerned with itself sought agreement and enlightenment through the rational-critical debate of private persons with one another flowed from the well-spring of a specific subjectivity. The latter had its home, literally, in the sphere of the patriarchal conjugal family.[14]

Habermas claimed that the coming together of private individuals as public was dependent on a traditional patriarchal, heterosexual private domain. It is a moot point as to whether Habermas inscribed that heterosexual patriarchy into the public or described it as he found it. What Judith Halberstam has called the "transgender moment" of the 1990s challenged that sense of the public sphere, only to see the very idea of the public disappear. The threat of an anti-homophobic, anti-racist, feminist public sphere was enough to retire the whole concept. As Reyner Banham realized in his study of 1960s Los Angeles, the place of public coming together is no longer the coffee house of the public sphere – who talks to strangers in Starbucks? – but the freeway. Here citizens are together but apart, debating with each other on talk-radio. Angelenos have long turned gridlock into recreation, although digital devices and cell phones have now made the car a place of work. Gridlock is now the quintessential (sub)urban experience, a badge of honor for those tough enough to take it. The public sphere was an important mental resource for the straight, white men for and by whom it was designed and it is therefore no surprise that we have heard loud laments from this sector at its passing. Why, Ivy league scholars lament, do Americans bowl alone? For the most part, the answer seems to be that they are instead driving their SUVs. The psychological sense of ease afforded by this mode of transportation outweighs such problems as pollution-induced asthma and the high death rate of luckless car passengers involved in accidents with SUVs. During the war, some celebrities in Los Angeles began driving the hybrid Toyota Prius, which does over 50 miles to the gallon, as a form of political statement.

For all that, there is a frequent expression of desire for nature and a regret for the passing of community. In the autumn, Long Island looks for nature at the pick-your-own farm, with the object of harvest being apples or pumpkins. Thousands of people engage in this activity, creating long lines of shining SUVs down once-country roads, displaying very urban sensibilities with their horns and parking techniques. While this is far from a new activity, its contemporary scope has far exceeded its former status as a sideline of farming. Now pick-your-own is a part of what is known as agri-tainment, a field that in the fall alone encompasses hayrides, pumpkin patches and haunted houses in derelict farm build-ings. Rather than seeking cheap apples, this is a culture desper-ately in search of nature, even if that means standing in a field to pick hybrid apples selected for appearance rather than taste, and liberally dosed in chemicals to keep away any trace of blight or insect life. Despite these efforts, the Latino farm workers who tend to the trees locate the practice in the global, rather than local, economy, with all the glaring disparities that implies. In a 1995 jeremiad against digital culture Clifford Stoll berated his readers: "During that week you spent on-line, you could have planted a tomato garden."[15] Somehow that anxiety has permeated into everyday life, but the result is not exactly what William Morris had in mind.

Wal-Mart America

Despite all this expressed desire for nature and community, superstore chains that obliterate traditional downtown or village shops continue to dominate Long Island's economy, often against people's better judgment. The giant of these stores is Wal-Mart, an all-purpose store that sells almost everything and at low prices. With an annual turnover of $250 billion and 138 million customers a week, Wal-Mart has become the largest private-sector employer in the United States with 1.2 million employees. In Texas alone, Wal-Mart has 163 supercenters – each of which is a 200,000 square foot emporium that combines a grocery store with a department store – 68 Sam's Club warehouse stores, and 52 regional stores.[16] By the simple tactic of piling cheap goods on unadorned metal shelves, sold by low-wage, low-benefit hourly paid workers in a so-called "big-box" – essentially a large climate-controlled shed – Wal-Mart has generated profit increases of the order of 18 percent a year for the past decade. In the second quarter of 2003 alone, it managed a 15 percent increase, despite the economic slow-down. One retail analyst has compared Wal-Mart to the Black Death: "The plague comes to your village, and everybody gets sick, but not everybody dies." That is to say, its success has forced even those stores that survive its challenge to imitate it or respond to it. In California, the mere announcement of Wal-Mart's plans to open stores has led grocery store employers to demand wage freezes and higher out-of-pocket expenses for health benefits from their staff, provoking a strike. Sweezey's, a Long Island department store that has been a feature of local life since 1908, was forced to close in 2003 because of the competition from chains like Wal-Mart, prompting a belated outcry. Grocery stores have tried going up-market but this response is not open to the once high-end electronics stores. With DVD players made in China now retailing at Wal-Mart for $39, down from over $600 in 1998, hi-tech is just another disposable commodity.

Wal-Mart is notorious for its poor labor practices and censorious attitude. It has long refused to stock CDs from artists it considers inappropriate – mostly African American hip-hop artists – and has recently withdrawn magazines like *Maxim* from its shelves as being indecent. On the other hand, Wal-Mart sells Christian literature and, where legally permitted, guns. In response to what it sees as hypocrisy, *Playboy* has appealed to Wal-Mart "associates," aka shop assistants, to pose for the magazine, while also running some sharp investigative journalism into the chain. Local communities often protest against the opening of new Wal-Mart stores, knowing that their arrival spells fiscal death for small stores. Wal-Mart is alleged to use its corporate heft to obtain advantageous prices from its suppliers and in any event sells at prices too low for small shopkeepers to match. It pays sales clerks about $14,000 a year, some $4000 less than comparable unionized employees, reducing costs still further. Since 1995, the federal government has issued at least 60 complaints of illegal anti-union activity by Wal-Mart.[17] In October 2003, Wal-Marts in 21 states were raided by federal agents who discovered illegal immigrant workers staffing the cleaning operations sub-contracted by the store. These workers allege that they were underpaid even by the low standards of such labor, were refused vacations or benefits, and worked twelve-hour night shifts seven days a week. A civil racketeering class action suit has been filed and allowed to proceed on behalf of these workers.

Wal-Mart's alleged refusal to promote women is being pursued as another class-action lawsuit that is now being promoted by a coalition led by a former Miss America, although beauty queens are not known as being one of the more radical groups in the

United States. In fact, over 40 law suits are pending against the corporate giant. So, knowing all this, why do people continue to shop there, given that withdrawal of business is always the most effective protest? Faced with a choice between principle and price, personal finances tend to win the argument for most people, especially those on low incomes. Further, the absence of pleasure in the big-box shopping experience marks a move away from a public culture of consumption, often seen in the critical literature as a feminine practice,[18] towards a privatized consumption within the home. Far from lingering pleasurably over the unexpected, or having one's eye caught by the surprising juxtaposition of goods as the display in an arcade or department store aspired to do, the big-box store reduces visual pleasure to a minimum. Goods are confined to packaging, bearing the dreaded label "some assembly required." For so thoroughly has the Fordist production line model of the economy come to an end that the consumer is forced to turn producer in order to finish almost every domestic product. Wal-Mart's own advertising never draws attention to its products or stores but only to its prices that are always performing a "rollover" downwards for the delighted spectator. In a place beyond even postmodern irony and cynicism, price is all and the consumer is offered no greater hope than the sight of a reduction. In these circumstances, it is scarcely surprising that the excursion into the commercial space is as brief as possible in order to return to the safely secured space of the home.

Meanwhile, the parent company of the famed New York department stores Macy's and Bloomingdale's saw its revenues decline still further in 2003, leading to a closure of a Macy's store in downtown Brooklyn. So what happens in the suburbs has ramifications for the urban environment as well. In fact, New York City is in fact becoming more like its suburbs all the time. The intellectual city depicted in Woody Allen movies has become a town dominated by the Barnes and Noble bookstore chain, with only the radical St. Mark's Books holding out. The great bookstore featured in *Hannah and Her Sisters* (1986) has closed and the marvellous Books and Co. uptown was put out of business by its landlord eager to cash in on the 90s rent boom. That landlord was the Whitney Museum of American Art. The academic bookshop Labyrinth was created and subsidized by Columbia University for fear that university press books might become unavailable in the city. In 1989, a Gap store opened in the counter-culture capital of the East Village, right on St. Mark's Place, sparking a storm of outrage. Now Astor Place sports a dismal K-Mart and Toys R Us. Times Square, the former playground of commercial and casual sex, is now anchored by the Disney play-of-the-cartoon *The Lion King* (1994), while video arcades and ice-cream stores have replaced the porn cinemas eulogized by Samuel R. Delaney.[19] New Yorkers are at least supposed to look different than their suburban cousins, hipper and thinner. A survey conducted by the city in 2003 found that 35 percent of residents were overweight with an additional 18 percent being obese, in line with national figures: so much for the stick-thin denizens of *Sex and the City*. At the same time, the 90s boom drove many young people and artists out of Manhattan to Brooklyn and even Queen's, making the city itself closer to a bourgeois utopia than it has ever been, at least until 9-11. With the end of the crack epidemic producing a declining crime rate and the ever-escalating real estate prices, Manhattan is now the perfect suburb that never was.[20]

The Hyperhouse

Long Island's emergence as a suburb during the post-war boom years was directly related to the defense industries. The suburban houses of that era were built using "pacified Second World War construction technology"[21] for workers and management involved in the defense industries created by the Cold War on Long Island. These houses were mostly single family homes on small plots of land, ranging from single-storey ranch houses to two-storey cottages known as Cape Cods and the larger colonials. The defense industries left or closed down in the 1980s and Long Island re-invented itself as a service industry economy, centered on new technology. A new wave of housing accompanied the economic revival in the mid-90s. The dominant architectural style of the vast new homes that have been extensively constructed in the past decade is a hybrid that one might call New England Victorian. It is designed to evoke the colonial past of Long Island, without forcing people to live in the small rooms of the Puritan salt-box house. This "dream house" architecture is actively and passively racialized. Simply by virtue of being suburban, the domestic house is coded as not non-white, regardless of the ethnicity of its inhabitants. In a more active sense, race and the uses of space have been intimately connected on Long Island since its white settlement. Long Island was relatively densely settled by indigenous peoples when Europeans arrived. War, the shame-faced "purchase" of Indian lands, and above all the devastating epidemics of alien diseases like small-pox meant that the native presence was drastically reduced as early as 1700, although the Shinnecock people still have a nation on the island.[22] With the displacement of the indigenous people, the island became mostly farmland. Its produce fed New York City but also the West India trade, meaning the supply of food to the enslaved in the West Indies. Most of that farming was also done by slaves, whose population numbered 33,343 in 1800. Some 13 percent of the 19,000 Suffolk County

Figure 1.5 The Hyperhouse

residents were African Americans at this time,[23] while one in every three residents of King's County, now Brooklyn, was African American, a higher percentage than in South Carolina.[24]

The canonical American painter William Sidney Mount (1807–68) included many African Americans in his scenes of Long Island farm life in the mid-nineteenth century. In some of these works, like *California News* (1850) or *Dance of the Haymakers* (1845), the African American figures are there to provide what pictorial theory has called "local color," a contrasting and perhaps exotic detail. But the figures are not stereotyped, although they stand at the edge of the picture space, along with an Amerindian figure in *Dance of the Haymakers*. In *Farmers Nooning* (1836), an African American farm worker is the central figure, sprawled in the sunlight on a pile of hay while three white farm hands sit in the shade. A white boy tickles the resting man's ear with a piece of hay. Certainly, the recumbent male figure, glistening with sweat, is an object of desire. But unlike the Neo-Classical painter Girodet who took pains to depict the Haitian revolutionary Jean-Baptiste Belley with a massive penis in his 1797 portrait, Mount decorously conceals the genital area from the viewer's gaze by raising the figure's knee. If the pose seems effeminate, the figure also has a mustache and is well-built. Given that the painting was made only nine years after the abolition of slavery in New York, while the peculiar institution was still in force throughout the South, Mount's painting is more noticeable for its lack of demeaning stereotype than the reverse.

Mount's painting was all the more unusual because segregation and racial violence have a long history here. It is a sorry tale, all too familiar to students of American history. The African diaspora presence on Long Island has left extensive, if often ignored traces. As early as 1708, enslaved Africans on Long Island rose in revolt and killed four whites. Babylon was the location of the first black baseball team in the United States, organized by Frank Thompson, the headwaiter at the then fashionable Argyle Hotel, in 1885. The team was soon known as the Cuban Giants and later played in the Negro Leagues. In 1917, an African American army unit, the

Harlem Hellfighters, had to be shipped early to France to prevent fights with racist white troops from Long Island. The Ku Klux Klan was so successful in recruiting Long Islanders in the 1920s that some 20,000 people in Suffolk County, 12 percent of the total inhabitants, were members at its high point. Cross burnings were regular occurrences in Babylon and neighboring towns, exploiting anti-Jewish and anti-Catholic sentiment. In 1923 a Klan rally in Islip drew 25,000 people and the 1926 Mineola Fair used a Klan rider on horseback as its logo.[25] In Lindenhurst, part of the town of Babylon, pro-Nazi German-Americans marched behind swastikas until the attack on Pearl Harbor forced them into an official change of view. The famous tract-house development at Levittown was so popular with white families, at least in part, because it was segregated. Most manual labor on Long Island is now performed by Latino and Chicano men, who line up on the streets for daily employment by contractors, landscapers and other service industries. Some locals have made their dislike of these newcomers plain, breaking into violence on two occasions. But for the most part, this is not a racism of violence but of the look, the gesture and the coded – or not-so coded – word. The intent is to maintain separation of ethnicities – equal perhaps, but separate certainly.

Although the homes serviced by this labor are determinedly "modern" in facilities, they invoke housing styles that are four centuries old or more. The typical 5000 square foot or more, all mod cons new house is centered around a Great Room named after the communal living space of medieval manor houses. This space was retained in the seventeenth-century English house that became the archetype of New England housing, as described in such texts as Gervase Markham's *The English Husbandman* (1613). Markham's ideal house included an open great hall within a Renaissance H plan and was very popular in the American colonies, for, in St. George's analysis, it "linked a backward longing for social hierarchy to the value of civic virtue in advancing capitalist culture."[26] This hybrid of form and purpose was also a key component of postmodern architecture, as first described by Fredric

Jameson in his analysis of the Bonaventure Hotel, Los Angeles, that is now the visual lingua franca in the suburbs. Just as the post-modern hyperhouse is distinguished from its urban and suburban cousins as a visualized modality of class, so did early modern settlers use housing as a means of visualizing ethnic hierarchies. In his 1625 account, Thomas Morton observed: "The natives of New England are accustomed to build them houses much like the wild Irish."[27] To see the Amerindian, the English had to go via an intersection with another colonial other in Ireland. Here ethnic distinction is always already implicated with other others. These associations could work in reverse. The English colonist Edward Howes, who missed the medieval great hall, saw both Irish build-ings and the indigenous wigwam as being analogous to them. But his very nostalgia made it clear that this was a question of a cultural anachronism between the modern English and the primitive Irish and Amerindians.[28] In the same way, the contemporary suburban house with "antique" details or features evokes nostalgia as a commodifiable value, while staking their claim to be new in terms of sheer size.

In the period of American colonization, a "play of metaphors linking the body and its death to buildings"[29] gave this mode of implication meaning. The great hall was seen as the center of the "housebody," such that the fireplace would be deemed the "heart" of the house, while the parlor, where the head of the household would sit, could be understood as its head. In all these complex corporal metaphors, one feature remained constant. The windows of the house were its eyes. As such they were both vital orifices and places of potential weakness. An opening of this kind presented an opportunity for witches and malevolent spirits to enter the house and corrupt its body. This anxiety remained palpable until the modern period so that Dracula, to take the most obvious example, made his entrance to Mina Harker's bedroom via the window. The contemporary suburban house, by contrast, makes sure that its windows are secure, usually by double-glazing. In the unlikely event that a window opens to the outside world, it will be guarded against insects and other intruders with fixed, locked screens. The windows rarely function in this traditional way, in part because the new hyperhouses are so often situated in proximity to major roads, whose noise and pollution needs to be excluded.

At the same time, circulation anxiety mandates that the house be inward-looking, rather than implicated with its others. Consequently, their eyes are "theatre"-style television screens, connected to stereo speakers, DVD players, a broadband Internet connection, and a video game device. These enormous 60-inch screens can only be accommodated in the Great Room of the new mansions, or in specially built entertainment rooms with the oxymoronic title of home theatres. These spaces are the most notable addition to the mansion-style suburban house since the elimination of servants' quarters, which led to the creation of a merged living-dining-kitchen area in the 1950s.[30] This series of interconnected living spaces are now given coherence by their relation to electronic media, rather than by the notion of "family" that was central to the suburban redesign of the 50s and 60s in the creation of "living areas." Now the house functions as the architecture for a local area network for film, television, voice and data, creating a thick web of cables around each building. So central to the function of contemporary homes are these media that the leading US electronics firm Best Buy has entered into a partnership with contractors and builders nationwide. This arrangement ensures that new homes will be built with the necessary digital cable and broadband Internet access to use top-end equipment. The new homeowners will then be encouraged to buy the necessary electronic goods from Best Buy. These screens are often the largest of a variety of screens in the house. A playroom is likely to have a television with a DVD/VCR for children's films, as well as a computer or video game console. Other TVs might be located in the kitchen or bedrooms with products being specially designed for each circumstance. The big screen is used for movies or television dramas that benefit from the large format. Soaps and other low-end productions can look bizarre in the life-size high-definition format.

This spectacle of private space found its ideal imaginary in the multi-image remote electronic format of the second Iraq war. Only a vast screen could properly accommodate the multiple images set against a digital image (a flag or logo) and mounted above a text "crawler" with the latest headlines. The thread connecting the American suburban house to the remote wars of the Middle East is less elusive than it might appear. Israeli architect Eyal Weizman has argued that on the West Bank suburban housing is a weapon: "The small red-roofed single family home replaced the tank as the smallest fighting unit." The red-roofed "Mediterranean" houses of the settlements identify the buildings from the air as Israeli, while also creating strategic "facts on the ground" and controlling the high points of the Occupied Territories. Just as American suburbia grew up around the military-inspired Interstate system of highways, so have these militarized Israeli suburbs integrated with a segregated road network for Israeli drivers. Research by the Israeli architectural group *Multiplicity* has shown that it takes an Israeli driver "ninety minutes to cross the West Bank from North to South, while the same journey takes a Palestinian driver eight hours – and this only on condition that the roads are open to Palestinian traffic."[31] When the watcher from the American suburbs looks at the news from the Middle East, they see their own past gone wrong. The militarized suburb in Palestine has failed to keep order in the post-Cold War world. This disaster is perceived as an active vindication of the "American way of life" that was held to be attacked on September 11, 2001. In this context, that means the transformation of the small-scale suburb as a weapon to a decentered network of strong points – the hyperhouses.

The hyperhouse has a multiple and complex view on the world via its various eyes that present themselves as being as invulnerable as the cyborg. It takes its place in the flows of corporal metaphor as a fortified body. Anthropologist Emily Martin has shown how the threat of AIDS and other new infectious diseases produced a new spin on the old metaphor of the body as a military machine. The image of a body at war with external enemies has been supplemented with a new idea of "the body as a police state." Martin analyses how the media coverage of science and medicine has increasingly depicted the body as fighting a war against insidious internal and external enemies, a measure of the flexibility of the immune system as it is currently understood. This flexibility echoed and supplemented the "flexibility" that is a key part of the global economy and a feature of the new warfare designed to fight against terrorism and rogue nations, using rapid, flexible response. In this flow of implication, the house becomes a body, which in turn can only be understood as a state at war. The military state at war is watched in that house, justifying its actions in language already familiar from the science section of the news. Pursued to its logical conclusion, the housebody as police state would be dictating to its residents what they should and should not watch in the manner of Rancière's police, for there is nothing to see except that which they want you to see. The new TIVO and Replay devices do exactly that, first recording multiple episodes of shows you like, and then suggesting and recording other similar shows. Parents use the device to offer their children non-stop animal shows rather than corrupting cartoons, while collecting the complete works of *Seinfeld* for themselves. With all this endless recording, who has time for the news? At the same time, the new giant houses are the preferred stage set for the new reality television dating shows from which all hints of exterior reality are rigorously excluded. As such, the hyperhouse is marketed globally as the new American dream. Failure on these shows is marked by ignominious return to ordinary life outside the house in one last trip in the stretch SUV.

The electricity blackouts of 2003 showed that the domestic security on which this flow of implication depends can be undermined in ways that have not been prepared for. In the early modern house, the main kitchen fire was understood to be the heart of the building and its heat, whether used for cooking or warmth, was the blood. In the contemporary house, electricity and gas are the blood of the housebody. The brief outages in the United States, Britain and Italy – all members of the so-called Coalition of the Willing – uncannily echoed the far more serious utility problems in Iraq.

Where Saddam Hussein restored basic services two months after the Gulf War of 1991, the American military are struggling to make any headway months after their declared victory. In considerable part this is due to the Iraqi opposition targeting utility supplies as an easy way to disrupt the country. The weekend after the electricity blackout in the US, water and electricity services were attacked in Iraq. It is not difficult to connect the dots, as many media commentators have already suggested: the next time someone wants to call attention to themselves in the United States, whether the domestic Unabomber/McVeigh variety or overseas terrorism, utilities would be the easiest target.

The vulnerability of the local housebody has become been part of the wider cultural web of implication since the 1979 classic horror film *The Amityville Horror* (1977). Amityville, by curious chance, happens to be located in the town of Babylon. Based on a sequence of scandalous events in 1975 and 76, the film put the early modern fear of the open housebody into national circulation. *The Amityville Horror* articulated some of the key terms for contemporary circulation anxiety. In 1975, a man named Ronald DeFeo Jr. murdered his entire family in an Amityville house. A year later George and Kathy Lutz moved into the house, only to be driven out ten days later by what they claimed was a series of paranormal events. The film followed a sensational book published in 1978. George Lutz was on ABC television in early 2003, still claiming his version of events to be true, despite widespread claims of a hoax. Needless to say, there are a slough of websites, for and against. I am not concerned with the "truth" of the events in Amityville but the way in which a culture of domestic anxiety was metaphorically expressed through the implications of a house in Babylon. In Stuart Rosenberg's film, when George Lutz decides to move into the house, he declares: "A house has no memory." The rest of the film, and this genre of recent horror cinema in general, is dedicated to refuting that proposition.

The house was late nineteenth-century Victorian, built with some traditional features, most famously the fanlight windows that Rosenberg established in the opening sequence as the eyes of the

Figure 1.6 The Amityville Horror
        (Courtesy of AIP/The Kobal Collection)

animated house. These windows are in fact a common feature of older homes in Long Island and are often repeated in today's hyper-houses. In the film's opening sequence, the house appears against a red sky, with only the windows fully visible, lit up devil red. The danger is transmitted sexually. George and Kathy are shown early in the film making love and, as all viewers of satanic horror films know, devils are highly sexed. George, however, soon becomes impotent. His sexual investment is with the house that takes him over at the expense of his business and his marriage. As Stephen King once pointed out, the spectator could identify with the existential and financial horror that home ownership can become, especially just after moving in. George becomes a double of the murderer and sees himself "reflected" in the satanic space that is later revealed in the basement with little devil horns. This doubling is an almost parodic invocation of Freud's theory of the uncanny, a term he explained by reference to a haunted house. If, as Judith Halberstam argues, "monsters . . . confirm that evil resides only in specific bodies and particular psyches,"[32] *The Amityville Horror* expresses a postmodern anxiety that such evil can be transferred from the housebody to the (post)human body.

The film makes sense only as part of a wider speculation about the paranormal and the domestic, on one hand, and within the sequence of horror films from *Rosemary's Baby* (1968) to the *Exorcist* (1973) and *Omen* (1976) series of the period. Indeed, Lalo Schifrin's score had originally been written for the *Exorcist* but was rejected and then simply recycled for use in *Amityville*. Elements of *Amityville* in turn entered the horror film vocabulary so that, for example, the flies that haunt the house when bad things are happening return in *The Ring*, a 2002 US remake of the Japanese horror film *Ringu* (1998), directed by Hideo Nakata, whose plot revolves around visual analysis. The story hinges on a video that is fatal to anyone watching it. In a detail specific to the American version, the peculiarity of the tape is visualized when a fly keeps moving after the tape has been paused. Later, Rachel Keller, the lead character, is able to pinch a fly out of the tape. What *The Ring*, and many other horror films since *Amityville*, suggest is that the boundary between the screen and "reality" is now permeable. At the end of *The Ring*, we discover that the tape kills when seen for a second time and a character leaps out of the screen to attack the viewer. It is perhaps no coincidence that the American version of *The Ring* plays up the permeable screen, whereas the Japanese film is more concerned with questions of the supernatural and paranormal. For it is in America that it has become clear that the new "eyes" of the housebody, its television and computer screens, are no more able to keep out evil than the old glass windows. As Slavoj Zizek has argued: "What happened on September 11 is that this screen phantasmatic apparition entered our reality. It is not that reality entered our image: the image entered and shattered our reality."[33] At the local level, the permeability of screen and image long predates the events of September 11.

Amityville plays with this question of boundaries as its central narrative feature. In a central scene, Carolyn, partner of George's business partner Jeff, visits the house, drawn by its "strong vibes." She has already discovered that, according to a book located by George in the local library, "it's all right here in history," claiming that the house was the site of devil worship in the seventeenth century. Carolyn's psychic powers lead her to the cellar where she is able to discern that the house is located on a former Shinnecock "exposure site" where "crazy people were left to die." George and Kathy Lutz did claim at one point that the house was situated on what they called a former "Indian asylum." Although they claimed to have evidence from the Amityville Historical Society archive for this asylum, it emerged that they had never in fact consulted it. The very idea of an "Indian asylum" is an odd one that may have been suggested by the nearby presence of the Pilgrim Psychiatric Center, a grim panoptic mental institution that held up to 10,000 patients in the 1950s. The absence of African Americans in the film accurately reflects the segregated nature of the town. North Amityville – outside the village limits – is a historically African American settlement first established by emancipated slaves. They and their descendants worked with and married Shinnecock and Montauket Amerindians. At the same time, Satanism in American cinema has often crossed ethnic lines. In *The Devil and Daniel Webster* (1941), the Beelzebub character, Mr. Scratch, justifies his claim to American citizenship in precisely these terms: "When the first wrong was done to the first Indian, I was there. When the first slaver put out for the Congo, I was on her deck."[34] There is an echo here of the Rolling Stones' classic "Sympathy for the Devil," matched by Halberstam's assertion that "within post-modern Gothic we are all of the Devil's party."[35] That is to say, given that the devil has been linked to ethnic, sexual and gender difference of all kinds, summarized in the figure of the monster, any form of modern rebellion based on difference will be, and has been, considered satanic.

The question of sanity and its borders runs through the film. Carolyn tells Jeff and George to stop being such "hyper-rationalists" and face the "facts" of what is happening. Defenders of the para-normal often insist that theirs is the only rational explanation for certain events. Within the film, simple acceptance is not an option. The Catholic priest Father Delaney declares himself to be a trained therapist but is dismissed by his superiors as suffering from halluci-nations. After he tries to hold a religious service of prayer for the Lutz family, he is confined to an asylum, unable to see or hear. This condition of safety with no unmediated access to the outside world is paradoxically the idealized utopia of suburban life. In the reality created by the film, the suburban house proper is a nexus of horror, diagnosed by Carolyn when she realizes that the basement conceals "the passage to hell." The early modern house had separated space above and below the "passage" between family-living space and space for servants, animals, cooking and so on. With modern building techniques this linguistic hierarchy became material and visualized, as basements became the place to which the necessary working parts of the house – furnace, electricity, gas and water con-nections, washer/dryer setups, tools and workbench – became confined. The basement is then what the seventeenth-century writers called the "fundament" of the house, both literally in the sense that it is the lowest point of the house and metaphorically as the anus of the house. The film points to the excremental nature of its occupying presence by having the toilets in the house overflow with black, bubbling liquid, perhaps brimstone. Once shown, this bizarre circumstance occasions no further comment in the film because it tells the viewers what they already know: that the house is satanic. In the closing sequence, the house bleeds, consistent with its representation as a housebody that refuses to sustain the private world that is supposed to take place within it. As George returns to the cellar to fetch the dog that has been, as ever, left behind, he falls through the stairs into a fundament of black brimstone. He emerges in the passage to hell, having been excreted by his own house, symbolized by his being covered in the black matter. George earlier has ranted at the unseen that this is "my house, my property" but, in the classic American nightmare, represented in films as various as *The Wizard of Oz* (1939) and *It's A Wonderful Life* (1946), it turns out that, after all, the housebody has been repossessed. Or, put another way, the house turns money to hellish excrement.

Amityville bequeathed this idea of a hidden entrance to Hell to popular culture. In the 1990s it re-emerged on television in a far more likely location, a high school. This gate to hell was of course that guarded by Buffy the Vampire Slayer. What made the series seem so right was the aptness of the parallel between high school and the entrance to hell, whether hell is understood as sexuality, adulthood, or the experience of everyday life in an American high school. Buffy, a high-school girl from Sunnydale, California, discovers that not only is her high school located over the Hellmouth, the entrance to Hell, but that she is in fact a Slayer, destined to combat the monsters, especially vampires, that come out into the human world. Following Marx, a number of critics have pointed out that capitalism itself is vampiric, sustaining its unreal life off the living labor of people. Capitalism, like the vampire, transforms materials from one thing to another. For the young Marx, "the *chimerical* nationality of the Jew is the nationality of the trader, and above all of the financier."[36] Following the implication, we discover in turn that the vampire was formed as a monster in terms predicated by nineteenth-century anti-Semitism, especially the notion of a parasitical drain on the body – whether the individual body attacked by the vampire, the housebody where he staged his assaults, or the body politic weakened by his depredations. Inevitably, the vampire also becomes a vehicle for exploring sexuality. As Judith Halberstam argues, the vampire is a "mechanism by which the consuming monster who reproduces his own image comes to represent the construction of sexuality itself."[37] As *Buffy the Vampire Slayer* matured, it accordingly developed a Gothic side that gradually took over the show. Willow, Buffy's confidante and a powerful witch in her own right, came out as a lesbian, while other characters explored different forms of sexuality via vampire-slaying. Buffy herself became the classic existential hero, doomed by her difference to lead but also to be alone.

After the school shootings at Columbine High School in another nearly all-white surburb, many politicians and journalists blamed digital culture for the violence. The shooters were held to be "geeks" wearing black trenchcoats that were supposedly derived from the movie *The Matrix* (1999). Many schools took precautionary measures against any recurrence by restricting geek activity. Jon Katz, a sympathetic journalist, opened a bulletin board at the hacker site slashdot.com for teenagers to comment. He was amazed to find that he was overwhelmed with responses to the site that he called "Voices from the Hellmouth" referring of course to Buffy. In a later account of these responses, Katz was moved to say that "geek" had become the equivalent of terms like "grrl power", "queer" and "nigga" – that is to say, formerly hostile names that had been reversed into affirmative ones by their objects. One poster to his site declared that: "Hellmouth has become the Stonewall for us geeks. It marks the point where we stopped running and hiding and waiting, and stopped and stood our ground. From this point on, we make our voices heard."[38] Stonewall, a bar in New York City, where drag queens and other gay men stood up to police harassment in 1969 and started the Gay Liberation movement, was an unusual comparison for a digital teen to make. Most of the posts detailed the ways in which "geeks" and "nerds" were persecuted in high school and the various revenge fantasies that the oppressed teenagers had dreamed up. These usually centered on the older, now fabulously successful geek driving an expensive car to a McDonald's take-out window, only to find that his (usual) server was one of the high-school jocks who had oppressed him. Others resorted to the Columbine route. In the summer of 2003, a teenager was arrested in Long Island, wearing a long trenchcoat and carrying an automatic weapon and thousands of rounds of ammunition. He claimed to have been inspired by the *Matrix* films to take revenge on his high school enemies. The student seemed sadly out of step with popular culture.

In its final series, aired in 2002–2003, Buffy was pitted in an all-engaging struggle against the First, the first principle of evil. The series seems to have wanted to deal with international events by staging Buffy in a showdown with the evil announced by the Bush administration to be the enemy, whether Osama bin Laden or Saddam Hussein. Like Satan in Paradise Lost, the First has the ability to change shape, gender and location at will. Buffy recruits, in effect, an army to combat the First. In the ensuing conflict, Sunnydale High School is destroyed and the Hellmouth is sealed. But having to destroy the town in order to save it has unfortunate echoes of My Lai and other failed imperial ventures. The new "eyes" of the housebody, its television and computer screens, are no more able to keep out evil than the old glass windows. It is through the figure of horror that the suburbs have entered the contemporary imagination whether in the recurrent nightmare on Elm Street, the gateway to Hell in Buffy the Vampire Slayer's Sunnydale, or the disavowing irony of the *Scream* movies (1996–2000). Despite its insistence on security, vernacular watching is in every sense a haunted practice.

It will inevitably be asked how this reading might be turned into resistance. But I am not sure that is the right question. Resistance is exactly what the police are looking for and it is in a sense that form of power that is called into being by the exercise of policing. I would rather think about how this sphere of circulation might give rise to a subjectivity that is not beholden to the police, which one might call anarchism. Such practice is a fascinating part of Long Island history. A utopian community called Modern Times sustained itself in what is now Brentwood from 1851 to 1864. The residents of Modern Times rejected the use of a money economy, printing bills allowing for an exchange of labor, and attracted a reputation for practicing free love.[39] Although long forgotten, Modern Times was featured in the 2002 exhibition *Fantastic!* held at the Massachusetts Museum of Contemporary Art.[40]

Interestingly, some very different critics like T.J. Clark and Sarat Maharaj have recently called for a reconsideration of anarchism, the space between the artist and Duchamp's "anartist."[41] Clark has gone so far as to say that socialism's epistemic crisis began with the break with anarchism in the 1890s, for which he has been soundly critiqued by scandalized Marxists in wealthy American universities. To look at 1890s anarchist concerns with race and racism, ecology and the politics of food, prison reform,

Figure 1.7 Jota Castro, *Survival guide for demonstrators*, 2003 installation,
   five aluminium foldable stands plus prints and booklets
   250 × 235 cm each, dimensions vary with installation
   (Courtesy of Gallery Maisonneuve, Paris)

and a decentered political system[42] is to get a shock of Benjamin's *Jetztzeit* (the time of the now). Anarchy also recalls the fashion, music and politics of 1970s punk that are again visible in suburban streets.[43] So to think of anarchism is not to disavow mass political action because that is the exception to everyday life, as in the recent anti-war demonstrations that were mobilized from people's houses via the Internet. That action was anarchist, in the sense of an action committed out of the sight of the police. It is intriguing in this context to recall that Eric Raymond's famous essay "The Cathedral and the Bazaar," one of the classic texts of digital culture, concludes with a passage from Kropotkin's *Memoirs of a Revolutionist*. It marks Kropotkin's turn away from a career as a government reformer to that of a radical and revolutionary. He had witnessed what he considered the failure of government-led reform in Siberia, but "to live with the natives, to see at work all the complex forms of social organization which they have elaborated far away from the influence of any civilization, was, as it were, to store up floods of light" that were to illuminate his subsequent career. In the passage cited by Raymond, reflecting that he had grown up in a slave-owning family, only to experience emancipation in 1863, Kropotkin came to

> appreciate the difference between acting on the principle of command and discipline and acting on the principle of common understanding. The former works admirably in a military parade but is worth nothing where real life is concerned, and the aim can be achieved only through the severe effort of many converging wills.[44]

That effort of many converging wills was what sustained the anarchy of the Internet before it was reined in by Microsoft and AOL. Seen more broadly, it is perhaps the first theory of everyday life as a form of resistance and as an alternative to centralized power, for all the nineteenth-century baggage of "civilization" theory.

The cybernetic hope of anarchic freedom was imagined as a cityscape by the Situationist architect Constant in the 1960s, that he called New Babylon. A Dutch painter who had come to abandon art in favor of the new practice of urbanism, Constant has a good claim to have invented the strategy of the situation. Inspired by his vision of a mass culture freed from the routine of subsistence labor by cybernetics, Constant imagined that automation would generate huge amounts of "so called free time." Rather than think of this time as "leisure," Constant and the other Situationists were inspired by the Dutch historian Johann Huizinga to think of it as play. Huizinga's theory of *homo ludens* – the person who plays – held that "play . . . is free, is in fact freedom."[45] In elaborating his theory of New Babylon, Constant quoted the cybernetic theorist Norbert Weiner who "compares the electronic machine to the imported slaves of antiquity." This new emancipation from the necessity to work would be for all, rather than the minority supported by slavery. It will generate "unprecedented freedom, an undreamt-of opportunity for the free disposal of time, for the free realization of life. . . . The freedom won as a result of the disappearance of routine work is a freedom to act," which he called the "lived work of art." In this society, traditional forms of art would be revealed as a "surrogate" for this kind of freedom.[46] New Babylon was to be the site of "the real practice of freedom – *of a 'freedom'* that for us is not the choice between many alternatives but the optimum development of the creative faculties of every human being."[47] Freedom was not to be seen either as an absence of constraint or as the self-ennobling choice among variables, which is presented by American apologists today, but as the possibility to play.

Constant envisaged New Babylon as a world without frontiers, which he called "a camp for nomads on a planetary scale," a vision that will be picked up in Section 3, in which I consider the migrant and refugee as a key symbolic figure of the new globalization that the Iraq war was designed to support. In fact, Constant's first work of this kind was an imaginary camp for gypsies, which he had designed in 1958.[48] Rather than an exclusionary camp that seeks to detain and deport the nomad, New Babylon opened a space for them to play as they chose without having to become settled to do so. These possibilities were emphasized at the level of the physical structures that Constant imagined for his project. The constantly changing spiral spaces were to be suspended above the ground, using modern materials like titanium and nylon, connected by ladders. Each area was allocated a color, such as yellow or red. The flexible building elements, lighting and environmental controls were designed to give the New Babylonians the greatest degree of experimentation.

This model was inspired by the old Babylon of the ghetto and marginal space: "these areas of the historical cities, where the outcasts of the utilitarian society stick together, these poor quarters where racial minorities, artists, students, prostitutes, and intellectuals are living together."[49] Situationism had always seen itself as a practice of the ghetto. As early as 1950 the Lettrist Gabriel Pomerand described Saint-Germain, the intellectual center of post-war Paris, as "a ghetto. Everyone there wears a yellow star above his heart."[50] This is of course a long way from the standard representation of the existentialist circles of Jean-Paul Sartre and Simone de Beauvoir. Rather it expressed the obsession that all the future Situationists felt with the old Jewish districts of European cities that had so recently been the scene of Nazi violence. Debord initiated a *dérive* (a random drift through a city) in the Marais, the old Jewish quarter of Paris in 1950. After running into a Yiddish argument in a bar on the rue Vieille-du-Temple, Debord and a companion were chased through the streets by some Hasidic Jews, only to escape by means of a staircase to the place Henri IV that the Jewish artist Camille Pissarro had repeatedly painted fifty years previously. It was precisely these kinds of intersections that created the atmosphere of Situationist "psychogeography," defined by Greil Marcus as an existing city "where building, route, or decoration expanded with meaning or disappeared for the lack of it."[51] One such space for Constant was the Jodenhoek, described by Andrew Hussey as "the Jewish quarter which had been almost entirely emptied of its population and been left to the city's human detritus, whores, drunks, drifters, before its reconstruction could be planned."[52] New Babylon was a ludic reimagination of this psychogeography, the dialectical other of the "living machines" of modern architecture.

In a curious intersection with this utopia of automated emancipation in the space of the ghetto, Norbert Wiener theorized the calculating machine, or computer, as "the modern counterpart of the Golem of the Rabbi of Prague."[53] The Golem was a proto-cyborg, a giant made of clay and supposedly brought to life to protect the sixteenth-century Jews of Prague by the magic of Rabbi Low. Wiener, whose father was Jewish, imagined the new machines as Golems, as feared by the Inquisitors of his Cold War era as the Black Mass.[54] Read retrospectively, and perhaps fancifully, Constant and Wiener might be seen as anticipating the Internet, whose endless twists and turns resemble New Babylon and the ghetto. But it was only after another opportunity to automate the basic needs of existence had been squandered in the digital boom, which managed to create *more* work for most people, that a disjuncture of the present took place in the re-exhibition at Documenta 11 after 30 years of Constant's defamiliarization of the present. Documenta is a quintennial exhibition of contemporary art held in Karlsruhe, Germany. In 2002, under the curatorship of Okwui Enwezor, it opened itself to global and digital currents beyond those usually represented in the art world. As a significant part of the show, New Babylon was an architecture of the present that is not present at the moment. At the same time, the fact that New Babylon, which claimed to be a new kind of liberated art for the masses, had to be shown in a traditional art exhibition was a kind of failure as well. If there is to be a response to the images of the war, it will begin not at ground zero, or even at the tabula rasa of decolonization, but in the (pre)history of Babylon, a metaphor for a present that is yet to come and a time that is out of joint. So now let's turn to what was seen from Babylon.

Section 2: The banality of images

In the second Gulf War, more images were created to less effect than at any other period in human history. Consider that the American networks CNN, MSNBC, and Fox News were broadcasting continuously throughout the six weeks of the war, as were the BBC, Sky and ITN news channels in Britain, al-Jazeera in the Middle East and many other networks worldwide. More journalists were present in combat than ever before, using all the advantages of new digital technology to transmit reports even as fighting was taking place. What was in retrospect remarkable about this mass of material was the lack of any truly memorable images. For all the constant circulation of images, there was still nothing to see. The relative anonymity of the war images must then be understood as a direct consequence of the media saturation. To adapt a phrase from Hannah Arendt, the war marked the emergence of the banality of images. There is no longer anything spectacular about this updated society of the spectacle. Colin Powell's presentation of spy photos to the United Nations notably lacked what has been called an "Adlai Stevenson moment," referring to the moment when the Americans documented the existence of missile bases on Cuba in 1963. The war itself offered the low farce of "Saving Private Lynch" and the staged destruction of Saddam Hussein's statue. It was ended, officially, with Bush's landing on the aircraft carrier *Abraham Lincoln*. All these events were literally re-runs: of *Saving Private Ryan* (1998), the revolutionary destruction of statues since

1776 and of the action film *Top Gun* (1986). They presented no visual drama comparable even to the CNN broadcasts from Baghdad in the first Gulf War or the film taken from falling "smart" weapons, let alone the dramatic film and photography of the Vietnam War or the Second World War. This is not to diminish the quality or quantity of human suffering in the invasion. Repellent images certainly abounded but sadly there has been no shortage of such material since Jacques Callot produced his series *The Miseries of War* in mid-seventeenth-century France. After Goya's powerful images of *The Disaster of War* (1808) in early nineteenth-century Spain, such work has been a continuous theme of modern visual culture. However, just as Sherlock Holmes once advanced a case by remarking that it was curious that a dog did not bark in the night,[1] so is this apparent lack of drama the key to an important story. For the absence of any dramatic images of the invasion was not simply bad luck or the result of censorship but rather the symptom of the changed status of images in the new mode of globalization generated since 1998. Images became weapons in the media war that accompanied and had justified the shooting war.

The striking accomplishment of the saturation of images gener-ated by the invasion – for all the notable exceptions and blindnesses – was that images ceased to be the subject of substantive debate. Any undergraduate in art history, film or media studies now arrives on the first day prepared to argue that the interpretation of images is subjective and socially conditioned. Given the intense divide and debate over the war, it would have been natural to expect a series of controversies over particular images or sequences. Surprisingly few such debates took place – despite minor skirmishes over al-Jazeera coverage of dead US soldiers and the odd debate over the photographs of Saddam's dead sons Uday and Qusay – and this absence was not without meaning. At the beginning of the digital era, when it first became clear that images were going to be manip-ulable, a moral panic was predicted. Journalists asserted that the public would cease to trust news images, knowing that they could be changed at will and a crisis of confidence would ensue. The war made it clear that only half of this prediction was accurate.

Certainly the global middle class is now accustomed to images being altered and they have probably done it themselves. But programs like Adobe Photoshop that make such changes possible usually advise their users that the various options available are simply digital renderings of darkroom tools. What has been learned, then, is that photographs and other representative visual media are all capable of distorting external reality and that they always have been.

This changed sense of the formal possibilities of visual media has not engendered the expected social crisis. Audiences all but expect photographs to be manipulated but are very quick to respond to allegations of textual fraud. When a *Los Angeles Times* photographer was found to have digitally altered a photograph of Iraqi war refugees for added effect, he was simply fired. But when a *New York Times* reporter, Jason Blair, was found to have invented reports and taken descriptions of scenes he claimed to have witnessed from photographs, the paper's editor-in-chief was forced to resign. The absence of visual panic does not mean that nothing has changed. It is now taken as read that all photographs in fashion magazines have been digitally manipulated. Readers discount for this distortion in their viewing of the images and other media outlets capitalize on it by showing deliberately dowdy photographs of celebrities. This self-conscious viewing allows the spectator to desire the six-pack abs on the front of *Men's Health* magazine, for instance, either as the external object of sexual desire, or as a presumptive self-image – or both – while providing a comfortable distance between the image and the real body of the spectator. This distance between image and perceived reality is the signature of the irony that has dominated Western mass media imagery for the past decade. The relentless commodity machine has generated a desire to escape all commercialization that is itself now being commercialized. A recent trend of this kind in the US has been for young people to avoid heavily promoted name-brand beer in favor of seemingly anonymous cheap brews like Pabst Blue Ribbon. Pabst capitalized on its very lack of status with "below the line" advertising, meaning promotions that are not visible as such or only to a select group. Soon enough the trend reached New York and from there the *New York Times* and away into redundancy. The point here is that "image" in all senses has been profoundly commodified. People use images as they do other commodities: as needed and without reverence, although they also have favorites among, and private uses for, all the different commodity-images available.

The weaponized image

So far so familiar. In 1967, in response to the first wave of such image-commodification, Guy Debord argued that modern life had become a society of spectacle that eliminated all sense of history. This spectacle was defined as "capital to such a degree of accumulation that it becomes an image."[2] Debord was extending Marx's argument about the formation of capital into modern consumer culture. In this view, money had been accumulated as itself in pre-capitalist society only to undergo a transformation into the abstract value of capital in industrial societies. Capital is not currency but an abstraction of value that seeks to perpetuate itself by growth. Debord argued that the next stage of development was for capital to abstract itself entirely from the process of production and become an image. The difference here is the difference between the Model T Ford and the Big Mac. The original Ford motor company, a classic symbol of modern capitalism, not only had no logo but also offered its customers only one choice of color – black – and for a long time, only one choice of car, the Model T. By contrast, McDonald's, the first symbol of US globalization, is nothing but its image. The famous "golden arches" have become immediately recognizable. The logo conveys far more than the identity of the premises. It promises a consistent and unchanging product for a low cost, a beacon of stability in a changing world for the harassed American workforce; or a symbol of change in economies newly subject to American domination. At the same time, the McDonald's logo lends itself to all kinds of parody whether visual or verbal. Poor-quality employment was referred to in the 1990s

Figure 2.1 McHouse

as a McJob, while the large-sized off-the-shelf house design of the period became known as a McHouse. Debord himself argued for such disruptions to the spectacle, which he called the *détournement*, or diversion. When the K Collective, a British pop-group/art collective, burned one million pounds of their own money, they enacted a *détournement*. The *détournement* provided the impetus for a wide range of contemporary art and social activism ranging from Barbara Kruger's advertising-derived art, to the Adbusters' parodies of commercials and the on-line satire of RTMark.com.

So given that audiences now have a day-to-day habit of questioning visual imagery, why was the Iraq war so visually uncontroversial? One answer can be found in the history of the self-styled "corporate sabotage" website RTMark.com (pronounced ArtMark and originally "spelt" ®TMark). RTMark's strategy has been to mirror the methods of global business, both by selling "shares" in their satirical enterprises, and by creating websites that use information supplied by corporations or politicians to expose their activities in an unfavorable light. These sites, such as their site for George W. Bush during the 2000 election campaign, use the corporate design style of their targets and offer no direct evidence that they are not official sites. Bush's campaign took strenuous exception to their action, calling it an abuse of freedom. However, in April 2001, an RTMark representative calling himself "Igor" pointed out at a New York conference[3] that their satire was now failing to have its intended effect. Through their subsidiary the Yesmen, RTMark maintained a site called GATT.org, a parody of the World Trade Organization. Repeated invitations to speak at financial conferences arrived until the day came that RTMark decided to accept. At a banking conference in Salzburg, a speaker calling himself Andreas Bichlbauer proposed that it should be possible for votes to be bought from people who did not intend to use them (see www.rtmark.com/yessalzburg.html). While his intent was of course to highlight financial corruption in the electoral process and to call attention to the high abstention rate in Western democracies, he was horrified to find that his audience treated his proposal seriously. At the peak of confidence in global markets to transform all they touched, no idea was too outlandish to be dismissed out of hand. The once all-pervasive postmodern irony no longer works as an effective tool of dissent.

Consequently, all the wartime cartoons and posters of Bush as a cowboy, so reminiscent of anti-Reagan images in the 1980s, failed to have any resonance. Bush actually gloried in the cowboy persona, asserting via Dick Cheney, that the (presumed) courage of the cowboy was required to meet the challenges of the day. It further reinforced the Republican claim to resurgent masculinity that had rendered Donald Rumsfeld, the defense secretary, into an unlikely sex symbol in 2001. McDonald's, perhaps the classic symbol of globalization, had seemed to be slipping in 2002 when it actually abandoned operations in three (unnamed) nations altogether. It tried to revive its fortunes by means of a new global advertising campaign using the tag-line "I'm Loving It." Outside the United States, this campaign featured retro imagery from the 1970s, a jerky hand-held camera style, and a youth-oriented feel that contrasts with its American image as a "family" restaurant. Despite the involvement of many young people in the anti-war movement and a sense that McDonald's is a symbol of the worst of American capitalism, these tactics were effective enough to raise profits by more than 8 percent in 2003, even as America came to be perceived as a major threat to world peace according to opinion polls.

As I suggested in the Prologue, the image has undergone a further stage of capitalist development and accumulation. If in the 1960s capital had become an image, by 2003 the image has become a smart weapon. Following Ernest Mandel's analysis of late capitalism, such a development might have been expected because it is precisely the existence of a "permanent arms economy" that has prevented capitalism from falling into a crisis caused by the tendency of the rate of profit to decline. That is to say, mass production tends to reduce costs so that any new product will become cheaper as a result of competition, causing profits to decline. Simplifying very broadly, Marx had predicted that this decline in profit would drive down wages and increase unemployment, bringing about a series of crises in capitalism. Mandel argued that the armaments economy continually intervenes in this process and changes its dynamics, accelerating the rate of technological change.[4] It is therefore not surprising that the intense pace of change in visual technologies during the 1990s, produced in part by military research, also generated a militarized form of the image. Consequently, the images of the war were not indiscriminate explosions of visuality but rather carefully and precisely targeted tools. There was no single agent of this design, although it was clear that a co-ordinated media campaign was planned and enacted by the US military and its allies. As Hardt and Negri have argued, it is one of the tendencies of the current form of globalization that its consequences appear to have been planned when they are not. Rather this was a convergence of medium and message such that each truly found itself for the first time.

The screens that were designed to receive these images, the large-screen theatre TVs of American suburbia, recognized them, so to speak, as friendly. On these screens, they did no harm. But to the opponent of the war, whether in the Middle East or the United States, these images were designed to overwhelm any response. Like the deadly videotape in *The Ring*, the weapon-image jumps out of the screen and annihilates its viewer. The strategy was different than that used in the film of course. Instead of a timed single attack coming one week after the first viewing of the tape, as happens in *The Ring*, the weapon-image overcame its opponents by sheer relentless persistence. So many images were being created that there was never time to pause and discuss any one in particular. As we shall see, a dramatic visual moment could be top of the news in one hour, only to be discarded to the dustbin of the present moments later. It is worth remembering that the strategy that saves the protagonists in *The Ring* is not the traditional horror film response of exposing the ghost's tragic demise and giving a proper burial to its corpse, for the tape continues to kill after this is done. What saves Rachel and her daughter is their copying of the tape, disseminating its image further into the mediascape. The only response to the weapon-image is to disperse it away from oneself, which in no way diminishes its overall power.

The weapon-image was delivered to our screens and newspapers by being "embedded" with the military. Formally, this meant that the technical support for the moving image was not the "dolly" of cinematic production, directly derived from railway technology, but the Humvee or, in some cases, the tank.[5] The "dolly" created the classic tracking shot of Hollywood cinema by mounting a camera on a platform that literally moved along a set of tracks. At the same time, it was also the principle of the production line in factories that moved partly assembled objects past workers who would attach another part to it in repetitive but efficient fashion. This mode of tracking has been replaced in recent years on shows like *ER* by the Steady Cam, a device that allows for a close-up and insistent intimacy of tracking in among the actors. The video camera on a tank with a real-time satellite link back "home" is the military equivalent of this viewpoint that Western viewers have come to take for granted. It embodies a stabilized and centralized viewpoint on globalization as the drama of the Western subject and its sufferings. Just as *ER* creates an imaginary Chicago where most of the doctors and nurses in a public hospital are white, treating mostly white patients, the war-cam represented a conflict in which Iraqi death and suffering took place out of shot. The very familiarity of the Humvee domesticated the images for American viewers and that familiarity reinforced their credibility. By the same token, this viewing platform from American armor made the images all the more questionable for anti-war watchers, especially for those outside the US. So when Private Jessica Lynch was shown being rescued in dramatic fashion by US soldiers at night, her heroism was instantly established. Accounts of her plucky resistance to capture and a daring rescue quickly dominated American media, assisted by her telegenic (white) appearance. Only it later turned out that Private Lynch had not fought back, was picked up with the active encouragement of Iraqi medical staff and without a fight. In fact, as a wave of media exploitation of her story broke in November 2003, Jessica Lynch dissociated herself from it, saying that too much was being made of her story at the expense of others who had taken greater risks or who had been killed.

The image became a weapon not just in the long-established sense of propaganda, but as something hard, flat and opaque designed in itself to do psychic harm. Throughout the war, military spokespeople talked about various assaults as "sending a message." Clearly, anyone beneath a 2000 pound bomb is in no state to receive a message. The image of the bomb being dropped sent a message within and without Iraq to the Baathist government and to the opponents of the war. It was for this reason that Iraqi television was suffered to remain on air throughout the US air assault. It was only when ground troops reached Baghdad that journalists became an American military target with the attack on the Palestine Hotel that killed two journalists. In fact, seventeen journalists had been killed by September 2003, which, compared with 300 US military casualties at that time, is a remarkably high figure. Al-Jazeera's Baghdad studio was also attacked and the message being sent was rather clear: do not report anything that the American military does not want people to see. The violence of the US assault was no surprise to Iraqis who had experienced the long bombing campaign of 1991 and the all but constant attacks in the "no-fly" zones since then. The target of these pictures – to be distinguished from the weapons themselves – was in part the global opponents of the war who had hoped that the structures of global governance were sufficient to translate their manifest popular will into a form of action. This spectacular bombing was a sign that the global rules of war and its civilized conduct – if that makes any sense – had definitively changed. Just as the financial revolution of the 1990s left the post-Second World War settlement of Bretton Woods dead in the water, so did the war and its declaration render the United Nations and its treaties on human rights null and void, at least for the time being. The affect and effect of a globalized culture that traffics in images are now fully apparent and they are intensely disturbing, even as the individual image loses its force. As the image becomes information, it loses the associations of remembrance and becomes nothing more than a tool of war. A confirmation of this weaponized status of the visual media came after the war, when Iraqis steadfastly refused to watch Iraqi Media Network, the US official television station, seeing it as simply more propaganda, despite the much-touted freedom of the post-war media.

In war, the image takes on a new guise. People do not suspend their disbelief in the truth of what they are being shown so much as subordinate it to the geo-political agenda of the nation state. It no longer matters whether the image is accurate, only whether it expresses a sense of the nation. The commercial image invites our participation in the image as a preface to consumption. To think about an advertisement, even critically, is to bring oneself to the edge of buying. The commercial image must remain open to debate, doubt and desire if it is to function properly. The war image, on the other hand, functions properly when its supporters simply accept it. To use the language of J.L. Austin, the war image is a performative event: it does what it says it is going to do, like a bride and groom at a wedding saying "I do." In that action, the marriage is done. By the same token, the war image performs the American victory as an image and it is done. One might say that the war image asks its viewers to pledge, not in sickness and in health, but "in truth and in falsity," the visual equivalent of the old tag "my country right or wrong." That is to say, there is no point in highlighting or exposing the oversights or mistakes in a given war image because the war watcher has already discounted them. The photographic historian Allan Sekula has argued that photographs are a form of currency, exchangeable and in constant circulation.[6] Following that through, the war image in particular comes guaranteed by the full faith and credit of the sanctioning government that allows it to be seen. It is an event that creates a sense of identification or disidentification. In short, the representation of war as global culture reconfigures individuals in history by means of visual images. Refusing that representation requires relocating both our sense of individuality and of history in negotiating visual representation. That such terms as "history" and "freedom," long part of the revolutionary vocabulary, have been so effectively co-opted by the global right indicates how significant they are as terrain for contestation.

In order to discredit the performative event of the war image, one would have to discredit the government that issued it, a tactic the Americans pursued very effectively by allowing the Iraqi Minister of Information Mohammed Saeed al-Sahhaf to continue to broadcast throughout the war. As his bold defiance came to be in blatant contradiction with what viewers were seeing themselves, the Iraqi government came to seem ridiculous. As a symbol of that process, the Minister of Information became a minor cult hero in Britain with a website devoted to his sayings (www.welovethe-Iraqiministerofinformation.com). The satirical send-up of al-Sahhaf as a buffoonish figure was mixed with a tinge of defiance against the American control of information. By the same token, many

American radicals turned to the BBC, the *Guardian* on-line and other international news sources for information during the war, feeling that their coverage was less biased. Indeed, the fact that there are now 2 million readers of the *Guardian* on-line in the United States has prompted the paper to think about starting an American edition. At the same time as American liberals were turning to the BBC for unbiased news, various British commentators excitedly denounced it as the Baghdad Broadcasting Corporation. After the war, BBC journalist Mark Damazer worried instead that the coverage offered by BBC World was too sanitized of death and destruction by comparison with other international coverage. His instinct was backed up by an analysis of BBC coverage that showed that it largely presented a pro-coalition viewpoint. The Australian government even tried to sue its own broadcaster ABC Australia, modeled on the BBC, for bias. There are some strong historical ironies at work here. During the Second World War, many resisters in Nazi-occupied Europe came to rely on the BBC to find out what was happening in the war. Now this pattern was being reversed. In a war that we were assured had all the moral authority of the war against Hitler, citizens of the "liberating" nation relied on their ally to inform them of what was happening. At the same time, media analysis ranging from the Marxist work of the Glasgow Media Group to David Morley's classic study of the audience for the BBC current affairs show *Nationwide* had been given a great impetus by the desire to criticize the BBC. The BBC was repeatedly characterized as conservative, overlooking cultural, gender and class difference in favor of a devotion to the establishment. The reliance placed by the US anti-war movement on BBC reports might be taken as a sense of how difficult their situation had become.

A good example of this difference was the fighting in al-Hillah, the small modern town closest to the site of Babylon. Consumers of Australian newspapers, Russian websites and Middle Eastern television would know that there was in fact a nasty encounter between US forces and Iraqis at al-Hillah. Perhaps because the first announcement came from the Iraqi Minister of Information, mainstream American media ignored all the reports of this fighting. All sources suggest that a contingent of Iraqi militia put up a fierce resistance to the 101st Airborne, possibly destroying one or more armored personnel carriers and wounding five or more on April 1, 2003. The response was a cluster bombing of al-Hillah. Cluster bombs drop, over a wide area, a large number of high-explosive bomblets that are meant to explode on contact but do not always do so, failing in 10–25 percent of cases, leaving attractive yellow canisters on the ground where they can be found by children. The International Red Cross reported that in the April 1 bombing, thousands of bomblets were dropped causing at least 280 civilian injuries and an estimated 33 civilians dead as well as many more combatants. Reports from Agence-France Presse and the Associated Press reinforced these figures with pitiful photographs of wounded children. After an initial denial, the US military acknowledged using cluster bombs in the area in an announcement dated April 2. By April 4, a sharp-eyed local journalist in St. Petersburg, Washington, had noticed the disparities in global reporting, a column that was posted to the *Seattle Post-Intelligencer* website. The *New York Times* offered only a skeptical account of Iraqi claims on April 3 and did not follow up by acknowledging the confirmation by US military.[7]

After the war had ended, the BBC followed up the attack and found that the cluster bombs had been targeted on al-Hillah itself, even though the pro-Hussein forces were outside it. Almost six months after the attack, on September 3, 2003, the town still looked like a war zone with shrapnel holes everywhere. The BBC reporter Paul Gilbert found one family who had lost all six of their children. No investigation had been made and certainly no comparable news reporting was offered to US audiences. After every major international event involving the United States, such contradictions in coverage are reported by media critics. In this case, it might help to explain why Tony Blair was in such political trouble over the justification for the war in the summer of 2003, while George Bush suffered a loss of a few percentage points in the polls. At the same time, the information is available to those prepared to seek it out, whether in print or on the Internet. While many people did engage in this relentless pursuit of information, others found it impossible to sustain the commitment to accuracy in the face of the relentless flow of weaponized images.

At the same time, there has been a concerted effort to keep the visual representation of death off Western television screens and front pages. Linda Williams, the film theorist, was quoted during the war as saying that the war coverage was in effect porn because it attempted to show the viewer everything that happened, in the manner of hard-core pornography. Certainly, the desire for panoramic vision was there. To pursue Williams' analogy, we might think of the network news as the equivalent of pin-ups, while cable news offered soft-core images, and only overseas news channels provided the odd glimpse of hard-core in the manner of a sex scene in a subtitled film. But, to follow Williams' own analysis, the war equivalent of the "money shot" (a porn industry term for the filming of male ejaculation) was carefully not shown, that is to say, death. When al-Jazeera did display the bodies of some dead Americans, there was a storm of protest, as if the dead military body has now become taboo so that its broadcast – rather than the violence of war itself – was the cause of the offense. The German novelist W.G. Sebald recorded that a teacher in postwar Germany "quite often saw photographs of the corpses lying in the streets after the firestorm brought out from under the counter of a Hamburg second-hand bookshop, to be fingered and examined in a way usually reserved for pornography."[8] For all the current fascination in American popular culture with pornography, no such interest in the corpses of dead Iraqis has manifested itself, while American dead are kept off screen even at their funerals and ceremonials. If this is pornography, then the war dead are a form of porn with which the audience is not comfortable, a degree of representation too far. While this new taboo does in part speak to the strategy of exalting the military, especially in the United States, it also reflects a deep-seated unease that there may have been something fundamentally wrong in the whole enterprise that could not therefore justify this loss.

Shell shock

War has the effect of rendering community out of the mass of individuals within the nation state. For those who choose to exclude themselves from this community, or who are radically excluded from it, there is a strong sense of alienation. During the period of the invasion of Iraq I noticed that those of us who had been opposed to the war were suffering from what I began to call war psychosis. For one friend its symptoms included a complete withdrawal from all news media and a re-reading of the collected works of Jane Austen, whose writing depicted an apparently more civil moment in human affairs (although the enslaved and colonized might beg to differ). Self-described moderate Alan Bennett, the British playwright, found that "the sense of impotence is what one never gets used to, of being led into ignominy and not being able to do anything about it except march and, one day, vote."[9] Other people were physically unable to watch the image of Bush on television or in newspapers. More common was a compulsive need to keep up with the news, scanning the various cable television news channels, on-line newspapers, weblogs, and other such media outlets in a desperate search for some kind of reliable information. Underlying that ostensible motive was the unspoken desire to find some evidence to prove the new imperial view of the world wrong. When the American army reached the outskirts of Baghdad, I predicted that the city would be taken in at most two weeks, a forecast that was greeted with disbelief by left-leaning friends. I was indeed wrong because it did not take nearly that long. Since the active invasion ended in May 2003 to be replaced by the war of occupation, the war psychosis has lifted even though the final outcome of events remains unclear.

The numbness, the despair and the depression felt by those who opposed the war as the invasion progressed cannot be attributed to the very predictable outcome of that stage of the conflict as such. Nor can it be linked to any support for Saddam Hussein, it should be added. Rather I want to suggest that it troubled our very sense of ourselves as "civilized" people, a term with difficult connotations of colonialism, missionaries and elitism at the best of times. Since the thesis of the "clash of civilizations" has become dominant in neo-conservative foreign policy circles over the past decade, the question of the nature of "civilization" has again become politicized in a very striking manner. In 1993, Samuel Huntington published an essay in the leading journal *Foreign Affairs* entitled "The Clash of Civilizations" that contained the kernel of this confrontational world view, in which the West is presented as facing an implacable cultural other: "As people define their identity in ethnic and religious terms, they are likely to see an 'us' versus 'them' relation existing between themselves and people of different ethnicity or religion." Huntington argued that Islam was going to become the source of an opposition to Western "civilization" that would define foreign policy in the early twenty-first century. While his ideas at first seemed extreme, especially to corporate interests in the Middle East, the events of September 11 and the highly influential neo-conservative group in the Republican administration led by Vice-President Cheney have combined to place them at the center of American politics. While opponents of the war rightly disclaim the "clash of civilizations" thesis, the idea of "civilization" cannot simply be abandoned to the right, although it might be better presented as the "cosmopolitan" or the "cosmopolitical." In this view, the cosmopolitan is a synonym for ethics, hospitality and a respect for difference, while being opposed to unilateralism and the assertion of one's own innate superiority (see Section 3).

If the destruction of the Baghdad Museum and National Library of Iraq, and the subsequent looting of provincial museums, libraries and archaeological sites, has come to be the most effective symbol of the waste that this war created, it provoked only a dismissive response from the US administration. Secretary of Defense Donald Rumsfeld notoriously dismissed the matter as a fuss over a few vases that were of no importance. While the Ministry of Oil was carefully guarded by US troops, nothing of value could be seen in an Iraqi museum from the administration's point of view. Apologists for the occupation have taken to asserting that there was no looting at the museum and, if there was, that the lost objects have been recovered. While some of the most famous pieces have been recovered, like the alabaster Uruk Head, together with a certainly significant number of other objects (c. 3500), a Pentagon briefing in September 2003 estimated between 10,000 and 14,000 objects were still missing from the Baghdad Museum. In addition there are serious losses from provincial museums and from unexcavated archaeological sites.[10] In the reductionist version of Huntington's already simplified thesis, Iraqi culture is a contradiction in terms and it is simply not possible for such a place to be considered central to human civilization as a whole. At the same time, the looting of cultural artifacts was permitted thanks to the dominant sense in the US administration that Mrs. Thatcher was right when she (in)famously remarked: "There is no such thing as society." If there is no society, then the notion of cultural property makes no sense because there is nothing that can own it. The state, which might be a substitute owner, is equally suspect for all functions other than defense. At another level, archaeologists who were quoted in the media regarding the importance of Assyro-Babylonian civilization to the human story and the writing of the Bible received hate mail and even death threats from outraged Christian fundamentalists, who denied the possibility that the story of the Flood, for example, was influenced by Mesopotamian legend. Of course, if you believe that the Bible is the undiluted word of God, known as scriptural inerrancy in fundamentalist scholarship, such influence is impossible. Needless to say, this constituency is a strong supporter of the Bush administration.

The widespread sense of depression I both observed and felt was, then, not a lament for the awful Hussein regime, which had long been opposed by the left while conservatives were supporting him against Iran. Rather there was a growing realization that the emancipatory promise of digital culture and an emergent global networked society in the 1990s had been for nothing, despite the recognition that the digital boom had been so relentlessly free market capitalist (see Section 3 for more on this). If there was to be any kind of revival of the social, let alone socialism, it would have to begin again, almost from first principles. In this sense, although the Gulf War was, to use the imperial phrase, a small one, it seems to have very broad cultural ramifications. The affect it has created recalls the disillusion felt by many intellectuals in the aftermath of the First World War. It is worth remembering that it was only in 1997 that global trade reached the levels it had attained in 1913. It was the experience of the First World War that convinced Sigmund Freud that there was a drive to destruction in the psyche competing with the drive to pleasure that he had earlier seen as shaping mental life. In his essay *Beyond the Pleasure Principle*, Freud surmised that a more "primitive" drive existed within the mental apparatus, summarized by the philosopher Arthur Schopenhauer in his estimation that death is the "true result and to that extent the purpose of life."[11] Despite his efforts to support his cultural thesis with neurological data, it was clearly the prolonged slaughter of the war that forced Freud to set aside his attachment to a forward-moving sense of history and to turn his attention to those forces within the individual that would allow for the repetition of unpleasant sensations, such as those experienced in shell shock. His celebrated observation of his grandson playing the *fort-da* (gone-there) game with a cotton reel to represent his "instinctual renunciation . . . in allowing his mother to go away without protesting" (page 14) led Freud to determine that the process of what he elsewhere calls civilizing involved more than the pleasure principle that he had previously posited as the basis of mental life. This story has overshadowed the still more specific game little Ernst devised to negotiate the absence of his father. A year later Freud noticed that the child "used to take a toy, if he was angry with it, and throw it to the floor, exclaiming: 'Go to the fwont!'" (page 15). While it is perhaps true that, as Freud suggested, the child was expressing his pleasure in having "sole possession of his mother," he was also using the war as a specific means of punishment. "Going to the front" would not just result in absence but most likely in death. In this sense, then, instinctual renunciation, or civilizing, is historically and culturally specific and therefore subject to change and intervention.

Uncanny Saddams

Among the various meditations in his later work that were inflected by his change of mind set out in *Beyond the Pleasure Principle*, in 1919 Freud wrote a short essay on the uncanny that has had enormous cultural influence. The essay mused on the contradictory term *unheimlich*, usually translated as "uncanny." Its various meanings depart from the general sense of "unhomelike," its literal translation, and lead to the paradox that Freud observed by which it also came to mean "homelike." As he meditated on the effects of the uncanny, Freud remarked that it generated "a doubling, dividing and interchanging of the self."[12] The haunted house was the best way that Sigmund Freud could later describe this affect that has been so central to the critique of modernity.

The uncanny image was noticeably central to the image war in Iraq, located above all in the images of Saddam himself. The war

Figure 2.2 Old Saddam
(Photo by the US military, courtesy CBS News)

began with an attempt to assassinate Saddam and throughout the hostilities there was official uncertainty as to his fate. American news media relied on such sources as a woman claiming to be Saddam's former mistress to discredit the photographs of Hussein being released by the Iraqis, by asserting that they were his doubles. To counter this position, the Iraqis released some television footage of Saddam in the streets of Baghdad on April 4, 2003. Far from settling the matter, the pictures simply provoked more questions. The media insistently questioned who was shown in the video and when it was shot. On CNN it was called "Picturing Saddam Hussein" as if proposing a visual culture conference on the topic of virtual reality. On ABC, digital analysis of circles of his skin as represented on the grainy video was held to reveal that the person seen was a double. Photographs of four supposed Saddam "doubles" were shown. On the evening of April 5 (East Coast time), MSNBC was running a story claiming that the film did show Hussein in the street but that it was taken in late March. The war damage and smoke in the background of the film were dismissed as, respectively, evidence of Baghdad's impoverishment under Hussein and the result of a test burning of oil. The idea that one would need to test oil to see if it makes smoke when it burns passed without comment in the war-fevered studios of cable television. At that moment, "breaking news" announced that Saddam and his sons had been killed (again) by a bombing in a Baghdad suburb. The "fixed" video story immediately disappeared from televised discussion and the print media that I saw did not pick up the discussion or comment on it. By morning the "definite" hit of the night before had been downgraded to a "maybe", of course, and the sons were no longer part of the discussion. The image stream flowed over the apparent mistakes and confusion, substituting the question of who had been killed in the suburban attack for that of the authenticity of the video without a pause. In part, this is an inevitable consequence of reporting in any war. Yet the extreme erasure of media memory and the apparent unwillingness to revisit any of these issues at a later date marked a new level of forgetfulness that cannot be described as trivial.

The uncanniness of Saddam's image survived the end of the war. When his sons Uday and Qusay were later killed by American soldiers, the administration was forced to release photographs of their bodies to quell suspicions within and without Iraq that these were not really Saddam's sons. Television reports showed Iraqis divided as to whether the bloated, bearded and blood-stained figures were the feared Hussein children or not. The hunt for Saddam himself continued with the release of several digitally altered photographs, suggesting what the deposed leader might now look like. These images were more comic than anything else and it was hard to imagine that Iraqis, who had been subjected to a barrage of images of Hussein for decades, would not recognize him in such feeble disguises. Again, the audience is in the West. Indeed, once he was found in December, 2003, Saddam was immediately recognizable despite his long beard and dishevelled hair.

What is intriguing in all this is to ask why Hussein's body became uncanny for American viewers. Its uncanniness was a consequence of the doubled Hollywood-style plotting of the war as a story. In the Hollywood action film formula, the complexities of the plot are reduced to a conflict between two leading men, often causing the villain to make mistakes in his pursuit of the hero. From the American point of view, this plot makes sense in interpreting the otherwise apparently "irrational" behavior of Hussein. This plot then intersects with that of the horror film in which, as every movie-goer knows, the monster proves remarkably hard to kill and keeps coming back from the dead. So was Hussein really the evil genius who is in effect the double of the hero, as many left critics asserted? Or was he simply a monster? If the latter, the plot would usually dictate that we locate and punish its maker, the Frankenstein figure. But as Saddam was so long the creature of the West in its conflicts with Iran that narrative line has not been pursued. As this war was already a sequel to the Gulf War of 1991, it is important for the monster to finally die so that the plot, as scripted in advance, can conclude.

With the real Saddam – or any of his doubles, who also eluded capture – refusing to play the part, the US Marine Corps drafted in a statue instead. In a carefully controlled media event, a statue of Saddam was toppled on April 9, 2003 to worldwide media coverage. A similar statue had been toppled in Najaf on April 4 and another in Basra by British troops on April 5, but these had only been photographed. The Baghdad statue fell on live television, in good time for the evening news. Edward Chin, a Marine from Brooklyn, first covered the face of the statue with an American flag and then hastily replaced it with an Iraqi one. Later that summer, Chin threw the ceremonial first pitch at a New York Yankees baseball game, as he seems to have become the symbolic American soldier. The flags were stand-ins for the hood used in hangings and it seemed that someone in charge realized that as the Iraqi flag was removed. With the aid of a tank, the statue fell and, whether by accident or design, was decapitated. A small crowd of Iraqis celebrated, while the global audience absorbed the resonances of this symbolic execution. New Yorkers had torn down a statue of George III in 1776, an action imitated by various French and Russian revolutionaries after them. In recent years, the revolutionary meaning of the act of toppling statues has been reversed as the socialist realist statues of Lenin, Marx and other heroes of communism were thrown down across the Eastern bloc. If that is the blueprint, then we have not seen the last of those statues of Saddam. Some of the Soviet-era statues, like the Moscow statue of Felix Dzhershinsky, founder of the KGB, have been replaced. In other places, socialist statues have become tourist attractions, as in Budapest where a park in which all the old statues were dumped is now a "must-see" stop. Can Saddam Disneyland be far behind? And will we have to read the Baudrillard book about it?

By the time US forces actually captured Saddam, there was a hint of anti-climax. Nonetheless the video footage released of Saddam's medical examination was striking and unusual. Showing a wild-haired figure, more reminiscent of King Lear than the comic-book evil genius he was cracked up to be, the short video sequence went into instant constant loop replay on all channels on December 13, 2003. A white, male figure, presumably a doctor, is seen depressing Saddam's tongue and examining his hair. This brief sequence demonstrated how the dictator, as he was endlessly called, was now no more than a patient, subject to US biopower. Biopower was Foucault's term for the intersection of life with power. That is to say, biopower is deployed when there is a medical and legal constraint on the living body, such as the age of sexual consent, the physical requirements to be a soldier or a police officer, or the visual capacity required to drive a car. It is by no means simply repressive or evil, therefore, but often constitutes the level of "common sense" in any given society. By representing Saddam Hussein in this fashion, rather than as a prisoner, the US military clearly intended to humiliate him. Certain responses in the Middle East played up to expectations. In the Palestinian Authority-controlled *Al-Ayyam* newspaper, Muhannad Abd-al-Hamid wrote that:

> Saddam's performance at the moment of his arrest and during his medical check was humiliating and appalling. This man, who had entered popular legend, looked . . . submissive, fragile . . . an Arab ruler who put his own personal security before any other considerations.[13]

In the United States, the always available commentators held that this capture had re-elected President Bush and disposed of the candidacy of Howard Dean. As these prophecies were very clearly in line with the wishes of their seers, a little caution might have been advisable. Soon rumors started to circulate, the most persistent of which had Saddam being captured by Kurds who then allowed the Americans to claim the prize. It may prove harder to dispose of the uncanny Oriental body than is immediately supposed.

The epic and the image

After the statues fell in Baghdad, I found myself wondering if the uncanny effect of Saddam's image was not a simple repetition from the recent past but a haunting of ancient origin. In short, was the ghost behind Saddam's head that of Babylon itself? Walter Benjamin, the German-Jewish intellectual, looked back on the First

World War from the perspective of the 1930s, and highlighted his sense that:

> A generation that had gone to school on a horse-drawn cart now stood under the open sky in a countryside in which nothing remained unchanged but the clouds, and beneath those clouds, in a field of force of destructive torrents and explosions, was the tiny, fragile human body.[14]

Benjamin was writing in his elliptical way about the decline of storytelling, remarking that "never has experience been contradicted more thoroughly than strategic experience by tactical warfare." He was puzzled to find that "men returned from the battlefield grown silent – not richer but poorer in communicable experience." Just as Freud could not explain shell shock by means of his theory of wish fulfillment, Benjamin wondered how so much dramatic participation in historic events seemed to have produced no wealth of stories. His musing was itself an uncanny forerunner of the problems encountered by historians and others trying to find out the stories of Holocaust survivors. Some events refuse to be told as stories. The story was being overwhelmed by what Benjamin even then called "information," although he was thinking of information in the form of print media. But if one drags, as it were, Benjamin's powerful image over those of the Iraq war, a means of thinking about what was seen begins to emerge. The immense surfeit of visual information during the war was conducive to the annihilation of effective narratives about what was happening. In the media, left and right alike were refighting the story of Vietnam – quagmire versus resolve to put it in the appropriate soundbite – but it was simply the wrong story in the wrong place. Iraq cannot be Vietnam for there is no Vietcong army or independent North Vietnam involved. By the same token, "resolve" alone, a codeword for real masculinity, has not so far produced solutions to the complex problems of rebuilding Iraq and creating a structure of governance. The images were fashioned to tell just one story. The embedded media told us bedtime stories with a single traditional moral, the old-fashioned triumph of Good over Evil. The messy reality of everyday life in Iraq refuses to tell such stories and cannot be shown. In short, if the world wars diminished storytelling in print and oral forms, the digital warfare of the past decade has now radically reduced visual narrative. Ironically, this elimination of narrative had been a goal of avant-garde cinema in the 1970s but has now been co-opted by the smart bomb view of the world.

Benjamin's sense of place and landscape suggests that one means of restoring meaning to these images would be to think of them as being within a certain mode of history, namely the epic. In what follows, I will use Benjamin's blend of historical research, theoretical argument and critical memoir as a guide through the inferno of contemporary everyday life. At the same time, I want to retain the sense of humility that I felt in that gym, knowing that what I knew was not enough to disrupt the violence of the image. Reading Freud and Benjamin together, there emerges in their essays a common concern with the cultural meanings and impact of death, rendered through the frame of Orientalism. Given the wholesale slaughter of the First World War, that is perhaps unsurprising. Interestingly for my purposes, both writers routed their narratives through the Orient, that phantasmatic Other to the West. Freud ends his speculative account with a quotation from the classic *Maqamat* (Assemblies) by the eleventh-century Arab writer al-Hariri (1054–1122), who lived and worked in the now-Iraqi city of Basra. Wittily and inventively written, al-Hariri's tale recounts the adventures of Abu Zayd, something of a rascal, in his voyages across the Islamic world from al-Andalus (Spain) to the Middle East. Freud's citation has another meaning in the present context: "What we cannot reach flying, we must reach limping . . . The Book tells us it is no sin to limp."[15] With the war-image dominating the air, the response must come from the ground and be grounded.

In Benjamin, the modern story is the diminished descendant of the Egyptian tales of Herodotus, fairy tales, and above all the incarnation of "epic remembrance" in *The Arabian Nights*, that product of Western Orientalism in the nineteenth-century translations such as the classic version by Richard Burton. For both writers the Orient served as a figure for death and dying. In the *Arcades Project* that Benjamin was compiling as he wrote his essay on *The Storyteller* in 1936, there is a section entitled "Ancient Paris." Benjamin made extensive use of the six-volume history of Paris by Maxime du Camp, a poet, writer, and photographer who traveled to Egypt with Gustave Flaubert. In this section Benjamin transcribed Paul Bourget's account of how Du Camp came to undertake his study. It happened that, entering middle-age, Du Camp found he required glasses. As he waited outside the opticians for his spectacles, he succumbed to a Romantic melancholy:

> Suddenly he began – he, the voyager to the Orient, the sojourner through mute and weary wastes where the sand consists of dust of the dead – to envision a day when this town, too, whose enormous breath now filled his senses, would itself be dead, as so many capitals of so many empires were dead.[16]

Then he came to imagine how interesting it would be to have an "exact and complete picture" of the dead empires of the ancient world. Death itself is Oriental, or more exactly, the Oriental is a *memento mori* for the Western imperial mind. As Du Camp waited to have his sight restored, death intruded into his visual field and created a new way to see the modernity all around him. Is it a co-incidence that in May 2003, a vast photographic project, sponsored by Olympus cameras and Adobe software, recorded the daily life of the United States under the digital boom title "America 24/7"?[17]

Further down the same page, Benjamin connects this Oriental vision of death with the specific location of Iraq in its former manifestation as Babylon. In a fascinating chain of quotations, Benjamin quotes Max Nordau, the theorist of degeneration, quoting Théophile Gautier, the art critic: "The modern Babylon will not be smashed like the tower of Lylak; it will not be lost in a sea of asphalt like Pentapolis, or buried under the sand like Thebes. It will simply be depopulated and ravaged by the rats of Montfaucon."

Babylon has and had a unique status as a place that is at once para-digmatically in the Orient but is at the same time modernity itself. The nineteenth-century metropolis imagined itself to be the modern Babylon, fascinated by its own decadence and haunted by its inevitable decline and fall. Babylon was the name given to the ancient within the modern that doomed that modernity to becoming ancient itself. This is Babylonian modernity, a fusion of the past and the present that creates a remembrance that was not there before. Babylonian modernity has now mutated into the aesthetic of cyberpunk, for Gautier's description of the fallen city is an uncanny anticipation of the wasteland of the future imagined by William Gibson and visualized in films like Ridley Scott's *Blade Runner* (1982) and the *Terminator* (1984–2003) series. In the political realm Babylonian modernity underscores the centrality of the region to contemporary imperial dreams, haunted as they are by the spectre of their own fall. Babylon is a memory of an ancestral past that is also a future that is yet to come. For the neo-imperialists, the legendary motto of the orator Cato to the Roman Senate "delenda est Carthago" (Carthage must be destroyed) has become rewritten as "Babylon must be destroyed." Power seeks to eliminate its history as a means of perpetuating itself, even to the extent of exorcising its ghosts.

"Information," mused Benjamin, "does not survive the moment in which it was new."[18] In the world of non-stop breaking news, ever-arriving email and incoming calls, information seems inescap-able. The Iraq war demonstrated that an excess of visualized information was incapable of surviving beyond its incarnation as "breaking news." Once broken, it was unusable. Against informa-tion, Benjamin posed remembrance, which you might expand to mean the epic mode of memory in its modern form. The ancient is retained within the modern as remembrance and thereby contains the promise of a future. In turn, the sense that the West is the proper home of modernity is also haunted by the memory of other urban civilizations that have risen and fallen. There are some dangers to such an argument. Given that Benjamin was an exemplary anti-fascist, we may set aside the abuse of the epic by fascism. However, the modernist image is often held to be anti-narrative and anti-theatrical, just as the postmodern is supposed to be opposed to all grand narrative. So when the art critic Clement Greenberg and other prophets of modernism spoke of the place of Oriental art as a precursor to the modern, they had in mind the abstract forms of Islamic art or "flat" Japanese prints that were made without using perspective. By contrast, Babylonian means of representation were fascinatingly hybrid in ways that are oddly familiar even as they are unthinkably different.

At the official end of the Iraq war, a new exhibition opened at the Metropolitan Museum of Art, called *Art of the First Cities*. It displayed astonishing treasures from the Fertile Crescent that, as so many accounts of the war noted, was the origin of civilization – if by civilization we mean living in cities. It was perhaps the most contemporary exhibition I have ever attended. The Ancient Mesopotamian statues and figures on display were all marked with the then new technology of cuneiform writing as if to play up the uncertain boundary between reading and seeing.[19] I couldn't help but be reminded of debates that have echoed round the academic halls over digital culture. The Internet in particular was claimed first for writing and then for the image when it is clearly a convergence of both media. Fancifully, I imagined the representation of a bulging net on the Stele of the Vultures (ca. 2550–2400 BCE) as the prototype image of the Internet. Turning to the monumental catalogue, I learned that this was the divine side of a stele, or monumental inscription, whose human side commemorated the triumphs of the Akkadian ruler Eannatum. The god Ningirsu is shown holding "a symbol, the lion-headed eagle grasping addorsed lions in its talons atop a net filled with defeated enemies."[20] If this is the Internet, then it is a more dangerous place than many have realized. In another representation of this net of enemies, the goddess Ishtar stands on the other side of the net. Ishtar is a goddess of love and war. Her radical alterity was such that, in Bahrani's analysis, "Ishtar is the place of all extremes; she is all that is in excess or out of control."[21] A space of love and war, torn between excess and martial triumph: now that begins to sound like the

Internet we know. A far less glamorous object from the same period as the Stele of the Vultures hints at the existence of a geek culture in Mesopotamia. A cuneiform tablet dating from ca. 2350 BCE displays a series of "composite signs for expressing large quantities in the sexagesimal system," that is, base 60.[22] Working up from 36,000 (60 × 10), the scribe finally created a sign for 12,960,000 by combining six uses of the sign that expresses (10×60^2), a number so large, he noted, that it "cannot be counted" – all of this without the idea of zeroes. The fascination with numbers in base form and what they can do is the abstraction that makes a digital culture possible by rendering information in base 2, that is, the famous zeroes and ones.

It then occurred to me that these analogies had been anticipated in Neal Stephenson's 1992 cyberpunk novel *Snowcrash*. *Snowcrash* imagined a not particularly distant future in which nation states – in particular the United States – had collapsed to be replaced by a patchwork quilt of franchised nations such as the Mafia's Nuova Sicilia or Narcolombia. In this chaos, the United States has become one rather unappealing franchise among many. There are no laws that apply to all franchises, known to the hackers in the book as burbclaves. The best diversion from this polluted, overpopulated and depressingly uniform landscape is the Metaverse, a kind of virtual reality Internet, wholly privately owned by a giant corporation that owns the fiber-optic network. Here people have virtual houses, clothes and personalities but, unlike William Gibson's earlier novel *Neuromancer* (1984), death in the Metaverse is not for real. This refuge is threatened by the emergence of a computer virus and drug called Snowcrash that reduces once mighty hackers to speaking monosyllables in "tongues," the Christian belief in religiously inspired universal language. To undergo a snowcrash is to lose the *cogito* and revert to an existence before the advent of history. To cut a long story short, it turns out that the owner of the Metaverse, one L. Bob Rife, has discovered that in ancient Babylon all people did speak the same language and were subject to control by the priesthood as a result. The legend of Babel represents, in this story, an actual historical event when the universal language was crashed by a cuneiform hacker. As the antidote to Snowcrash is found in a hitherto unknown cuneiform tablet, the novel is a pre-emptive condemnation of the loss of thousands of such tablets in the looting that followed the end of the Iraq war. Stephenson suggests that we need to be every bit as careful of our cultural DNA as our biological environment. So rather than represent Babel as a disaster, Stephenson sees it as liberating, opening up the space for binary thought that will eventually and inevitably create the computer: "Babel . . . moved us from a materialistic world to a dualistic world – a binary world – with both a physical and a spiritual component."[23] It would no doubt be churlish to point out that in a sexagesimal system as used by the Babylonians, dualism would have made no sense. Instead, let's recall that it was the Baghdad mathematician al-Kawarizmi, the inventor of the word "algebra," who introduced the Indian numeral zero to the West in the eighth century. And zero really did make a binary culture possible.

The horror of eternal return

This disturbing sense of a return from the past is what both Benjamin and Nietzsche, in their different ways, called the idea of eternal return. The question of recurrence lies behind Freud's uncanny as well, for there is nothing more prone to return than a ghost. The eternal return is the presence of death in life and of unseeing in seeing. The return undercuts all narratives, especially those of progress and triumph. In his *Arcades* project, Benjamin came to the subject via the apparent detour of boredom. Boredom, in his view, was a product of the mechanized and stultifying rituals of mass production, on the one hand, and its corollaries in the formal tedium of elite society. It was not for nothing that his two avatars in the nineteenth-century world were Charles Baudelaire, poet of Bohemia, and Marcel Proust, chronicler-novelist of the fall of the aristocracy. As Benjamin mused on boredom, he wondered what its antithesis might be. I would tentatively suggest that contemporary boredom has found its antithesis in horror and terror. Horror is the represented form of the dominant political affect of our time, terror. The Benjamin of our day must browse in horror films. In fact, the eternal return was, as philosopher Gary Shapiro has recently emphasized, always a visual moment: "What recurs in recurrence is the *Augenblick*, the twinkling of an eye or the moment of vision."[24] Nietzsche's Zarathustra thus asks: "Is not seeing itself – seeing abysses?" Shapiro reads the passage in terms of Hitchcock's classic film *Vertigo* (1958). One might go further and suggest that the constant return of the horror within each horror film, and its subsequent seeming eternal return in sequels, is the feuilleton of our times, chronicler of our boredom and fear alike. Benjamin, I like to think, anticipated this, writing:

> In the idea of eternal recurrence, the historicism of the nineteenth century capsizes. As a result, every tradition, even the most recent, becomes the legacy of something that has already run its course in the immemorial night of the ages. Tradition henceforth assumes the character of a phantasmagoria in which primal history enters the scene in ultra-modern get-up.[25]

Anticipating both the shipwreck movie and the supernatural horror, Benjamin understood that it is only through the most modern of guises that the eternal enters the contemporary. Being a regular patron of the Grand Guignol horror show in Paris during the 1920s, Benjamin was well placed to see the potential of modern popular culture to express the eternal return of the ancient.[26] From Frankenstein's use of electricity to create his monster in the 1938 film, via the depiction of American family life in *The Texas Chainsaw Massacre* (1974) to *The Ring*'s (2002) device of a permeable video screen, the horror film is always the place of the contemporary.

Interestingly, the film historian Miriam Hansen has argued that the Babylonian sequences in D.W. Griffith's classic *Intolerance* (1916) – which Walter Benjamin may well have seen – served to "convert the relative anarchy of the marketplace into a hierarchy of present over past."[27] The film is an interwoven narrative of four clashes between Love and Intolerance, beginning with a fantastic re-working of Babylonian history at the time of Cyrus' capture of the city in 539 BCE, continuing with the story of Jesus, the massacre of the Huguenots on St. Bartholomew's Day, 1572, and the modern story of the Mother and the Law. The enemies of Love, then, are the Babylonian priests of Bel, the Jews, the French and the feminists. The past episodes are rendered as precursors to what Griffith called "the ever-present, realistic, actual now," meaning the American now. The episodes were linked by a recurrent motif of a mother rocking a cradle, with lines from the Long Island poet Walt Whitman: "Out of the cradle, endlessly rocking" and "Endlessly rocks the cradle, Uniter of Here and Hereafter." Whitman's line could be read either as an evocation of endless return, or of a pro-gressive narrative, and, in very American fashion, the film struggles to resolve the motifs of progress and recurrence. Part of that incoherence stems from Griffith's attempt to use the charge of intolerance against his own critics, who had critiqued his 1914 feature *Birth of a Nation* for its (appalling) racism and defence of the Ku Klux Klan. While Babylon is presented as a historical experi-ence to be transcended, the film's ambiguities also suggest that it is a part of the historical present that must be negotiated.

Eternal return, then, is the constantly feared antithesis to the American narrative that is still grounded in nineteenth-century notions of progressive history. When politicians speak of America as the "indispensable nation," or the "lone superpower," or as a "force for good" they are all implicitly deploying the theological narrative of progress in which Babylon has been destroyed and must always be destroyed, a motif that was inevitably literalized by the usual websites. Seventeenth-century Puritan discourse imagined heaven to be "a City of Habitation," a perfect city without material flaws.[28] This apparently obscure reference is central to contemporary American conservatism, following Ronald Reagan's parting evocation of America in Biblical terms as a "shining city on a hill." The widespread description of 9-11 as America's loss of innocence was greeted with a good deal of impatience in other parts of the world. How could a nation, it was asked, built on slavery and genocide, the agent of so many wars, be considered innocent? It was precisely in this sense that America had not been subject to the abyss of eternal return but was alone struggling to render the progressive narrative of theological history. What was at stake in the solo strategy of the Iraq war was retaining that sense of American uniqueness. Many European nations make their relative lack of power a major talking point in public discourse, an unbroachable theme in American politics. Ralph Waldo Emerson codified this idea into two notions of history. One is of the earth, bound by facts and data, while the other is spiritual:

Time dissipates to shining ether the solid angularity of facts. No anchor, no cable, no fences avail to keep a fact a fact. Babylon, Troy, Tyre, Palestine, and even early Rome are already passing into fiction. The Garden of Eden, the sun standing still in Gideon, is poetry thenceforward to all nations. Who cares what the fact was, when we have made a constellation of it to hang in heaven, an immortal sign?[29]

Understood in this ambiguous context, American policy since 9-11 has been so impervious to factual critique because such details are held not to matter. What is above all at stake is America's isolation from the law of eternal return that began, as Emerson notes, with Babylon. It is the very inevitability of the devastation wrought by the passing of time that inoculates American particularism from Babylonian modernity, just as the theory of historical progress is opposed to that of eternal return. It is an illogical system that cannot on its face be troubled by facts or images. But the inevitable undercutting of that system is anticipated within itself, finding its mirror in Babylonian modernity. Rather than persist in trying to make the modern image of the Iraq war attest to its own culpability in our own time, which it is designed not to do, I want to read them against this ground. Now it seems that rather than Emerson's confident Republic, America is closer to William Faulkner's vision of the defeated South where the past isn't even past, let alone over.

Babylonian modernity revisited

Babylonian modernity began, predictably enough in 1789, the year of revolution, when the French scholar de St. Croix presented a *Memoir* on the ancient site to the Academy of Inscriptions in Paris. Babylon was described as the city of the Biblical prophets Jeremiah and Isaiah, a vast metropolis of 25 streets, each fifteen miles long and 150 feet wide that went in straight lines to the 25 gates of the city. Each of these gates was made of brass, defending a city that, according to the prophet Jeremiah "Hath been a golden cup in the Lord's hand, that made all the earth drunken, the nations have drunken of her wine; therefore the nations are mad" (Jeremiah, chapter 51, verse 7). Within the city was the temple of Bel, which, according to de St. Croix, had no statues in it, as if respecting the (supposed) Jewish prohibition against graven images. Its fall was taken by ancient and modern writers alike as a comment on the cyclical nature of power and the inevitable decline of the apparently insuperable. These comments must have had interesting resonances in the Paris of 1789 as the Bastille was stormed and the National Assembly claimed its right to be a representative assembly of the people. Anticipating Benjamin and the Romantic reverie on the decline of cities, de St. Croix wrote that: "Man builds in vain; he seems to labor for nothingness [*pour le néant*]. How many cities have been, the very names of which have been forgotten?"[30] When Claudius Rich, a British agent of the East India Company, arrived on the site in 1811, he was predictably more prosaic in his assessment:

> From what remains of Babylon, and even from the most favourable account handed down to us, there is every reason to believe that the public edifices which adorned it were remarkable more for vastness of dimensions than elegance of design, and solidity of fabric rather than beauty of execution.[31]

The grandeur of Babylon's layout was irresistible for at least one American tank commander from the 101st Airborne, according to a Reuters report dated April 9, 2003. He drove his tank through the archaeological site of Babylon, perhaps imagining himself to be Nebuchadnezzar or one of the other legendary rulers of the metropolis. He was quickly ordered away for fear of negative publicity. But US planners had no hesitation in staging their handover of control in the area to Polish troops at Babylon in September 2003, despite the fact that 60 percent of Poles opposed the move.[32]

This ceremony was staged at the rebuilt amphitheatre of Alexander the Great, a site the *New York Times* confused with that reputed to be the Tower of Babel. Perhaps the imperial setting was supposed to reflect on the nascent Polish army rather than the obviously still dominant American forces. The transfer of power from Americans to Poles, a transfer that took place in nothing but name, was held to enact a "diversifying" of command. If it was believed to have taken place at the Tower of Babel, the site of the original confusion of language, it was also an occasion of eternal return. Polish troops came under mortar fire at the unironically named Camp Babylon from their first day, so they have taken to displaying signs identifying themselves as Poles, not Americans, and flying the Polish flag in the hope of deterring their attackers. Babylon has been no place of refuge for these latest recruits to Fortress Europe for the first Polish combat death since the Second World War occurred in November, 2003. At the same time,

Figure 2.3 US troops hand over control to Polish forces on the site of
ancient Babylon, modern al-Hillah
(Courtesy of REUTERS/Peter Andrews)

Polish prime minister Leszek Miller celebrated Poland's national day at Camp Babylon and has used the Polish alliance with the United States to press his claims to a greater presence in the European Union, even as Poland has received very few of the contracts to rebuild Iraq. As it was Poland's opposition that led to the failure to ratify the new European constitution in 2003, Babylon is now playing a part in the politics of modern Europe.

The one aspect of Babylon that did appear in the American media was Saddam's reconstructed palace at the site. This edifice displayed the tawdry extravagance he seemed to have associated with splendor. Indeed, the ancient Assyro-Babylonian Empire was a constant source of reference for Saddam's rule, although he never seems to have realized how that might in fact have told against him. The streets of his cities were built on the huge scale of the old empire, making them extraordinarily vulnerable to attack by armored vehicles. Despite this knowledge, there was a good deal of meaningless speculation in the American media about street-fighting in Baghdad in the early days of the war. A full-page layout in the *New York Times* early in the conflict visualized the imagined drama for its readers.[33] The *Times* converted to gung-ho patriotism as soon as hostilities commenced, creating a special section called *A Nation at War*, a close echo of its title of the section *A Nation Challenged* that was published after 9-11. In this repetition, the paper of record implicitly endorsed the assertion that Iraq was connected to al-Qai'da, which was so extensively believed that one poll found some 70 percent of Americans thought the hijackers were Iraqis acting on Hussein's orders. In October 2003, Bush finally acknowledged that the administration had no evidence that there was any connection. In the *Times*, the street-fighting to come was illustrated by a computer-generated drawing, credited as being derived from official US army publications. It showed a narrow street edged with houses in poor repair at uneven angles to the cobbled roadway. Captions highlighted the irregularity such as the following description of "surface areas": "Streets, alleys, parks, fields that follow natural terrain and are broken up by manmade features." A sheet hangs from a window, indicated as a tactical marker but also an index of poverty for most *Times* readers, accustomed to the spoken and unspoken rules of suburban life that forbid hanging laundry out to dry. The sheet Orientalized the street plan as a place of dirt and poverty.

Maps and satellite photographs published in the *New York Times* on preceding days had clearly shown the grid pattern of Baghdad, transected by major avenues and boulevards, rather than the represented maze of alleys. What the drawing not so subtly set out to do was remind viewers of the Orientalist cliché of the Middle Eastern city as a tangled web that reflected the irrational thinking of its people. As the British governor of Egypt Lord Cromer wrote in his account of the country, published in 1908: "The European is a close reasoner . . . The mind of the Oriental, on the other hand, is eminently wanting in symmetry."[34] In the article accompanying the drawing, General Wesley Clark – later to run as an anti-war candidate for the Democratic Presidential nomination – anticipated that "the Iraqis will want to fight close and dirty . . . The fighting will be full of the tricks we have already seen and more: ambushes, fake surrenders, soldiers dressed as women, attacks on rear areas and command posts." The dirt of the street indicates the "dirty" tactics that are to come from the Iraqis, who, like all Orientals, are inherently untrustworthy. Clark cited the "outrage" of unnamed American commanders at "such dishonorable tactics," complete with a photograph of Mogadishu to remind readers of the *Black Hawk Down* incident in 1993 when nineteen Americans were killed in Somalia. In Ridley Scott's 2001 film of that name, the alleys of Mogadishu were represented as precisely the dangerous, unpredictable Orientalist maze that the page-spread was trying to evoke. At the same time, the viewpoint of the soldiers in the street was familiar to many as that of first-person shooter video games. In this fertile blend of Orientalist cliché, historical and political resonance, connections to terrorism and association with Hollywood entertainment, the *New York Times* presented its readers with a mythical enemy capable of inspiring fear and disgust. This mode of representing the "Oriental" at once insists on the impossibility of internal change and that the

"Oriental" is incapable of representing himself, whether culturally or politically.

Imagining Babylon

The modern Western response to Babylon has never been favorable. On the basis of observing the surface rubble and a few random digs, Rich ranked Babylon below the Egyptian pyramids and even the Aztec temples of Mexico. This view seems not to have been altered by any subsequent discovery, as if the Biblical condemnation of Babylon mandated that its art must be inferior. When Austen Layard discovered the astonishing winged lions at Nimrud in 1846, he wrote acidly that "altho[ugh] the sculptures of Assyria show a wonderful *comparative* knowledge of the arts, when the time and country of their execution are taken into consideration, they are undoubtedly inferior to the most secondary works of Greece or Rome."[35] Perhaps one can only find what one is looking for. Ironically, Rich found something else that he was not interested in at the time: "Bitumen flows out of the ground at Babylon . . . The fragments of it scattered over the ruins of Babylon are black, shining and brittle, somewhat resembling pit-coal in substance and appearance."[36] Of course this bitumen, also known as petroleum, was the surface sign of the oil wealth that leads Western nations to take such a keen interest in Iraq's domestic affairs. In the nineteenth century, bitumen was used as a pigment by modern painters, striving to find dramatic blacks for their Romantic canvases of *Sturm und Drang*. One artist who made use of the new color was Eugène Delacroix, who created one of the most famous Orientalist representations of Babylon in his vast canvas *The Death of Sardanapalus* (1826). The painting shows a scene from the poem by Lord Byron in which the Babylonian king Sardanapalus watches with calm detachment as his city is sacked by invading Persians. The action depicts the interior of Sardanapalus' chambers, where servants are putting his horses to death, while others hang themselves, as the king looks on. The bitumen darkens the canvas, creating a gloomy and rather hard-to-see painting. The Orientalist pigment had its revenge on the Orientalist painter because, as it never dries to solid form, variations of heat cause it to expand and contract, leaving extensive cracking on the surface of the paint.

Sardanapalus' calm resignation and refusal to fight prefigured the apparent Iraqi response to the American attack. In a sense, Iraq became figured as a modern Sardanapalus, cruel, lazy and effete at once. US marines frequently expressed their contempt for the Iraqi "cowards" on television. An NBC news report for April 5, 2003 described how black-uniformed "Sudanese and Syrians" put up a much harder fight, delaying them for a day. There were supposedly 25 of these men but how their nationality was established in the middle of a firefight was not explained. The report raised them up as proper fighters unlike the cowardly Iraqis but nonetheless labeled them "terroristic," taking their black clothing alone as evidence. Such uniforms were also worn by the *fedayeen*, the Iraqi militia who were reported as offering the fiercest resistance. But these fighters could not be called Iraqis because on American TV, Iraqis were all Sardanapalus, reclining on a divan as their servants and slaves are put to death. It is not my suggestion that news reporters or marines were actually thinking of Delacroix's painting but rather that the artwork stands for and condenses centuries of official and popular discourse about the Orient, such that it has become all but "common sense." Orientalism flows around us like a river.

Rich knew that bitumen had been used by the ancients to secure their bricks and there is some Protestant disdain in his writings for the laziness of making do with what comes to hand rather than striving to build properly, that is to say, in the British way. Bricks were nonetheless his point of identification with Babylon. The Babylonian burnt brick was taken by Rich and others as concrete evidence for the Bible story that records the building of the Tower of Babel with burnt bricks. As Rich pointed out, the standard translation of Genesis that read "slime they had for mortar," was a mistranslation for bitumen. His discussion involves Hebrew, Arabic, Chaldean and Latin in a very matter-of-fact way that demonstrates the peculiar paradox that an immense range of knowledge was required to produce the labored, racialized clichés of Orientalism. Rich expounded on the bricks at length as they were the only Babylonian artifact he came into contact with:

> They are of several different colours; white, approaching more or less to a yellowish cast, like our Stourbridge or fire brick, which is the finest sort; red, like our ordinary brick, which is the coarsest sort; and some which have a blackish cast and are very hard.[37]

In the deserts of Mesopotamia, the Orientalist envoy found the image of London's brick terraces in the 2000-year-old Babylonian brick. Scholars now agree that brick was a central and dynamic technology of ancient Babylon, reaching its peak with the glazed bricks used to decorate the famous Ishtar gate, now in Berlin.[38] The brick was also a place to write, as Rich noticed. Ironically, this point was not lost on Saddam Hussein, who had all the bricks of his reconstructed palace at Babylon inscribed with his name and that of Nebuchadnezzar.

Graphic epics

Benjamin believed that to be epic, a story must involve the "soul, eye and hand." A hand-made brick with a written inscription in cuneiform meets that requirement. Where might it be found today? I would like to suggest that the graphic, especially the graphic novel, is one place of the epic. Drawing of course classically involves the hand and the eye. The soul becomes involved when the drawing moves beyond similitude to narrative. In a certain sense I realize that this sounds like the classic definition of History painting as prescribed by the Academies of Painting. But the graphic novel, even at its most serious, is now more fun and more effective than History painting, despite the recent efforts of critics to revive it. The Situationists used the graphic format in the 1960s, making posters by rewriting the speech bubbles in appropriated comics to promote their radical ideas. The most recent incarnation of the graphic has developed in response to Art Spiegelman's 1991 classic *Maus* that, appropriately enough for our purposes, imagined his parents' ordeal in a Nazi concentration camp and its subsequent effect on his own life in a two-tiered world of humans and animals. Spiegelman's lead was followed by Joe Sacco, who investigated life in the refugee camps of Palestine in a nine-part series of comics that were later collected to form a substantial work.[39] Sacco sees his work as journalism but it works in a far more compelling way than the standard news report. Over the series, what is perhaps most telling is the seeming endlessness of it all: endless cups of tea, tales of woe, attacks by the Israeli army, the ongoing resistance of the first intifada, leading to more attacks, more death and so on. The documentation of Israeli arrest without trial or even charge at camps like Ansar III, which in November 1991 held over 6000 inmates, makes it clear that Palestine was perhaps the first territory to be subjected to the detain-and-deport regime of the empire of camps (see Section 3). For all the documentation and description that Sacco offers – including Israeli points of view – the pages that stayed in my memory were a double-page text-free depiction of the Jabalia refugee camp. Sacco visited Palestine in the winter so rather than the effects of heat that Western readers might expect, we see the camp after prolonged rain. Deep puddles and mud suffuse the scene, recalling other camps at another time. Children step gingerly through the mess on the way to school, past abandoned vehicles and some horse-drawn carts delivering sandbags. Movement is still further impeded by barricades built from oil-cans by the Israeli defence forces, trying to prevent the hit-and-run tactics of the intifada. Overflowing garbage is piled up everywhere, food for the dogs. Telephone wires straggle across the crowded alleys, reminding us that this is in fact part of the developed world. All of this, Sacco says, can be seen on a tour arranged by the United Nations Relief and Works Agency for Palestine. He even gives their phone number. When Sacco periodically leaves the occupied territories to recuperate in Israel, the reader feels a sense of relief from the constant tension, only to realize that it is precisely this freedom that is not available to the Palestinians. While some will seek to dismiss his work as propaganda, Sacco addresses the questions of Islam, the treatment of women, and anti-Semitism without seeking to present the Palestinians as Western heroes. He ends the book with a representation of an Israeli soldier questioning a boy, who is forced to stand in the cold rain. He concludes:

> If I'd guessed before I got here and found with little astonishment once I'd arrived, what can happen to someone who thinks he has all the power – what of this – what becomes of someone when he believes himself to have none?

That boy in the rain would be 24 or so now, if he's still alive. The second intifada in Palestine has been led by young men of his age, who have taken the terrible step from the stone-throwing of 1991 to the suicide bombings of the present.

From the other side of the gender divide in the Middle East, the Iranian author and artist Marjane Satrapi explored her childhood either side of the Iranian revolution of 1979 in her two-part graphic novel *Persepolis*. Drawn in a deceptively simple black-and-white series of small frames, three rows to a page and between one and three images each row, Satrapi's novel effectively conveys the complexity of personal, familial and national history in Iran. She grew up in a well-to-do but leftist family, descended from princes, although her personal hero was her communist uncle, later executed by the Islamic government. It is in exploring these forms of complicated implication that Satrapi's novel is most effective. First published in French in 2000 and 2001, *Persepolis* is full of prophetic ironies when read in 2003. The Iranian revolutionaries are shown tearing down a statue of the Shah in front of two modern tower blocks. A man who looks like Marji's (as she is known in the book) father orders: "Pull a little more to the left."[40] Yet her father also effectively blocks the romance between his servant and a neighbor's son, justifying his action by saying: "In this country you must stay within your own social class." Satrapi places these contradictions in front of the viewer without judgment, showing that the relationship of the private and the public is always more complicated than political theorists would allow.

The drama in the book is not only that of the Islamic leadership, which Satrapi shows to have been always contested within Iran, but also the war with Iraq. After the Iraqis bomb Tehran, Satrapi draws Marji sitting with her feet on the coffee table, yelling in boldface letters: **"WE HAVE TO BOMB BAGHDAD!"** Her father points out that the government has imprisoned all the pilots so that any retaliation would be impossible. In a classic adolescent tussle, Marji takes a patriotic stance to distance herself from her father. When the television suddenly starts playing the old national anthem the whole family is overwhelmed. Marji's father insists on checking the official news that Iran has in fact attacked Baghdad with the BBC news, much like US anti-war protesters in 2003. When the BBC announces the Iranian raid, Marji and her father dance around the table and her mother suddenly appears smaller in size, as if she was a little girl, marginalized from the celebration of the adults. This subtle evocation of the psychoanalytic undertones to the family debate over patriotism is not addressed by the characters or the narrator but emerges through the drawing itself.

As the war with Iraq continues, Satrapi describes how boys from working-class districts were recruited into the Iranian army aged fourteen with the promise of attaining paradise, should they be killed in action. They were given plastic gold-colored keys to take into battle, which, they were told, would open the gates of paradise. In a powerful page, all the more effective because of its contrast with the standard layout, Satrapi highlighted the class divide within Iran. The top two-thirds of the page comprises a stylized drawing of a group of young boys being blown up in the war. The Futurist style of the explosion alludes to the similarities between the Iran–Iraq war and the First World War, which in effect created Iraq. The figures of the boys are black outlines and the only detail that can be seen is the little key around each of their necks. In the bottom frame is a depiction of a clandestine punk rock party attended by Marji at the same time. She was wearing a sweater full of holes and a necklace made of nails, both created by her mother. The chapter ends with the lapidary line: "I was looking sharp."[41] The Iranian government refused a peace settlement, insisting on maintaining the war until the Shi'ite holy city of Karbala was taken. New official graffiti appeared on city walls, encouraging further sacrifice. One read: "To die a martyr is to inject blood into the veins of society." Satrapi visualized the slogan as a stylized, vaguely Egyptian, figure lying in abstract space in seeming agony with lines of blood pouring into its arms. A full page drawing of the war follows which Marji "enters" from top left down a staircase, saying "They eventually admitted that the survival of the regime depended on the war." After our eye travels across a scene of hand-to-hand fighting, again reminiscent of the First World War, she exits at bottom right through a door, concluding: "When I think we could have avoided it all . . . It just makes me sick, a million people would still be alive."[42] Such figures are so literally unimaginable that the far smaller number of casualties of the World Trade Center seems more real. By creating a visual framework that draws on the ancient art of the region, Arabic calligraphy and decoration, and Western figurative realism, Satrapi creates a space in which this subject can be addressed and imagined. Death on such a scale is epic indeed.

So too was the disaster of 9-11 and it has found a graphic artist in Art Spiegelman, author of *Maus*, whose characters recur in his new series *In the Shadow of No Towers*, written in the aftermath of 9-11. Spiegelman, who lives in downtown New York, was one of many who feared for his own life on that dramatic day. His subsequent work has tried to reconcile that fear and the emotions it inevitably engendered with his political outrage at the Bush administration's response. As the series was being written and published, Spiegelman publicly resigned from the *New Yorker* magazine, asserting that its editorial policy was overly favorable to the administration. The *No Towers* series is remarkably visually and intellectually sophisticated. In the segment published in the *London Review of Books* of August 7, 2003, Spiegelman used five different visual styles, each offering a different form of response to the continuing peculiarity of living in a city that is now defined as much by what is missing as by what is there, even as that sense of loss is exploited for political ends with which many New Yorkers radically disagree.[43]

Rather than review the entire series, which is not yet complete at the time of writing, I want to examine these five visual moments. In the left-hand column, were the double-page spread a newspaper, is the title graphic. It shows a pigeon thinking of one of the World Trade Center towers, rendered in a *pointilliste* series of colors that conveys the imminent destruction of the building as well as making it far more beautiful than it ever really was. Spiegelman's caption read: "I saw stunned pigeons sitting listlessly on the pavement in Lower Manhattan for *days* after the explosions on 9-11. . . . right under the surface we're all still just a bunch of stunned pigeons." This is an observation worthy of Kafka or Benjamin and most people would have made it the subject of an entire piece. But Spiegelman carries the thought through with admirable self-examination. In three horizontal strips across the spread, a narrator challenges other New Yorkers not to continue in this dazed sleep. He is represented sitting up in a wide bed with eight other sleepers, depicted in sepia caricature, reminiscent of Goya. The narrator worries that perhaps his anger is misplaced: "Maybe it's just *my* little world that ended . . . But then I glance at the news and there's absolutely no doubt . . . *THE SKY IS FALLING!!!*" There's a comic-book reference here to the Asterix series in which the Gauls, forever resisting the Roman Empire, are afraid of only one thing: that the sky may fall on their heads. We're also reminded of Goya's famous print, *The Sleep of Reason Produces Monsters*, suggesting that the public should be doing more to oppose what is being done in its name. This shout of fury settles the narrator down to sleep, even though the other sleepers are now wide awake and afraid. Third is a literally interstitial strip, retelling a New York anecdote, done in black and white, as if to evoke Woody Allen, the city's unofficial cinematographer. The four-frame strip shows a young woman telling a story about being mugged on Avenue C (once the dangerous borderline of the city, now home to a white bohemian scene). The punchline is: "I was, like, sooo relieved! Things are finally getting back to normal!" The most substantial segment has a subtitle: "Weapons of Mass Displacement." Spiegelman uses Freud's notion of displacement – that a traumatic subject is displaced by the unconscious to another seemingly innocuous one – without explanation for a city still dominated by therapy and even psychoanalysis. Suggesting that America attacked Iraq as a displacement for al-Qai'da, or that domestic guru Martha Stewart's alleged minor infraction of insider dealing rules has taken the symbolic place of Enron and Halliburton, Spiegelman reserves his worst rage for NYC Mayor Michael Bloomberg's decision to ban smoking in all bars and restaurants, read as a displacement for the anxiety about air quality after 9-11. This last anxiety has in fact been validated as a recent study has shown that children of Manhattan residents who were *in utero* at the time of the attacks are physically smaller than average. This political analysis is rendered visually compelling by Spiegelman's surrealist drawing in which his head alternately changes place with a lamp shade, his hand holding a cigarette and his shoe. Finally, the artist metamorphoses into his character from *Maus*. In the fifth and final panel, the "Most Wanted" deck of cards issued by the Americans in Iraq is parodied as The Architects of Armageddon, featuring Ashcroft, Rumsfeld and Bush, "available wherever finer petroleum products are sold." This work is graphic in all senses. It deals with anxieties related to death and dying, war, and corrupt politics, while telling jokes, making witty and artistic references and presenting a pungent political argument.

The sophistication of Spiegelman's drawing style is in interesting counterpoint to a successful cartoon-strip in *Rolling Stone* called "Get Your War On." Created by David Rees, the strip uses characters derived from the "clip-art" now available to all computer users, whether supplied with Microsoft software, as in this case, or on the web. The ability to create graphic-enhanced documents reached its apogee in the days following 9-11, as the residents of the city with perhaps the highest concentration of computers in the world churned out thousands of "Missing" posters in full color with photographs and carefully edited layouts. Rees' strip refuses to use the visual excess available from the imagery of the war so that his powerful text stands out all the more. These banal images are as empty of content as a weaponized image. But it is also important to note that without the images, the text would lose this enhanced impact and become a series of angry jottings. It is only by this strategy of presenting voided images that the text gains density.

A 2003 collection of comics from the Israeli Dimona Comix [sic] Group shows that the medium has come into play in expressing the alienation and anxieties of Israeli citizens in the current crisis. Dimona is a new collective of young graphic artists who publish their work in English to facilitate international attention. Their first collection appeared in January 2003. Only one story directly addresses the security situation but the mix of surrealism, psychedelia and a Kafka-esque transformation of a person into a praying mantis in the others, suggest a culture in which everyday life feels radically out of joint. Two stories out of five deal with the experience of being fired, one combined with the end of a personal relationship, suggesting the economic and personal price of the intifada. Ifat Cohen's story "Nearly Noon" describes a crisis in the life of James, a loner shepherd, told from the point of view of his "inner voice." James' search for simplicity is undermined when the sheep become transformed into messengers from urban society. He rejects them as "industrialized sheep. Pathetic messengers of Babylon." With the help of the inner voice, James resists the blandishments of Babylon. Cohen's visual style is intense, mixing decoration and psychic imagery with text to place considerable demands on the viewer/reader. By contrast, Guy Morad tells a spare, sparse version of a day in "August" as experienced by an Israeli-Arab man, called Khaled. After negotiating roadblocks to work, he is fired. His daughter Mira calls to make plans for her wedding and he cannot tell her the news. On the way home, his car is thoroughly searched by Israeli police. His day ends with him contemplating the view of soldiers on patrol in the moonlight, still unable to tell his family what has happened. Here the overwhelming presence of the police drowns out not just politics but the possibility of privacy, perhaps even of that inner voice which constitutes the Western sense of personality. The hope here is that somehow telling this unadorned story in English might constitute a means of bringing the crisis to international attention that could initiate some change.

Pursuing the difficult freedom of remembrance through the graphic medium is a strategy that was familiar to Walter Benjamin. Although he was later criticized for it by Frankfurt school colleagues like Theodor Adorno,[44] Benjamin saw something epic in the very sparseness of drawing. After a conversation discussing Mickey Mouse with friends, including the composer Kurt Weill, in 1931, it seemed to Benjamin that "in these films, mankind makes preparations to survive civilization." The Mouse proved that it is possible to survive, even when the body no longer appears human in any way. In this sense, Benjamin had a sense of how representation might move beyond the anthropometric and the mimetic, an issue that has all the more powerfully returned in our own era of digital manipulation. At first Benjamin thought that the mode of story-telling in animation was a radically new disavowal of experience but he soon corrected himself: "Not since fairy tales have the most important and most vital events been evoked more unsymbolically and more unatmospherically." In this way, "the public recognizes its own life" in cartoons.[45] These cartoons were the early animations that did not yet imitate the viewpoint of the film camera before Disney became the American dream factory. Benjamin saw something of the epic in these cartoons that allowed the public to recognize its own conditions of existence.

There are pre-figurations in these notes of the dramas of our own time: the hybridization of the human body and the cybernetic machine, the crisis of the visual image caught between weaponization and everyday life, and the very notion of the "civilized" in the West. For Benjamin, the graphic cartoon was a location in which vernacular watching could engage with the complex conditions of everyday life, just as the graphic novel does today. The crisis of indexicality that was once seen as being an issue for photography in particular has become a drama for the mimetic image in general. That is to say, the "reality effect" in cinema, photography and television is suspended, as indicated by the plethora of staged events presented as "reality television." The graphic is not a simple solution to the complex and networked problems of the contemporary any more than it could destroy 1930s fascism, but is rather a symptomatic intersection of these dilemmas. It resonates because its intersections between a certain mode of high art, the popular comic book, and critical writing seem to allow an epic encounter with the present, so that a disjunctured temporality can emerge. Such encounters are necessarily fleeting, like Gilgamesh's visit to the underworld, but they can mark a point of departure. The argument is not that because of the weaponized image all discourse should be conducted in graphic novels. It is that the opacity of those weaponized images forces our glance sideways and around them. In astronomy, averted vision is used to try to see dim astral bodies that elude the central part of the eye. In thinking through eternal return in everyday life, Benjamin was drawn to the tragic figure of the revolutionary Auguste Blanqui, ending his life in prison by completing a book called *L'Eternité par les astres* (Eternity via the stars), in which he imagined multiple worlds co-existing in the same moment, musing that "everything one might have been actually is in another world."[46] As Oscar Wilde, another refugee in the panoptic prison, remarked: "We are all in the gutter but some of us are looking at the stars." There were stars painted on the highest ceilings of the ziggurats in Babylon.

Section 3: The empire of camps

What, finally, of Babylon as the global order of capitalism, the Babylon of Rastafari? The experience of African diaspora in the Caribbean has generated a number of syncretic religions such as Santeria and vodun, but Rastafari has become perhaps the best-known through its exponents in reggae music. Rastafari takes its name from its spiritual leader (or, in some versions, divinity) Haile Selassie, sometime king of Ethiopia. Born Ras Tafari in 1892, Selassie was taken to embody Biblical prophecies of a black monarch from Africa. Rastafari is not simply a cult, however, but a means of negotiating the complexities of the African diaspora experience. It emerged in Jamaica during the 1930s as part of a series of struggles against the British colonial government for adult suffrage and local rule, culminating in the achievement of suffrage in 1944 and independence in 1962. For Rastafari, "Babylon" is a complex, multivalent term that expresses both a sense of personal alienation from society and the historical experiences of imperialism and slavery. It connects the Jewish exile in Babylon to the Roman Empire via New Testament language describing Rome as Babylon. With this link between Babylon and Western imperialism established, Babylon in Rastafari has become "the primary symbol for the interpretation and assessment of the colonial establishment."[1] At the same time, Babylon is what the Rastafarian intellectual Dennis Forsythe has called "the first-person, gut-level experiences of alienation and frustration under slavery, colonialism and their legacies."[2] Finally, and perhaps above all in everyday life, Babylon means the police, the local enforcers of colonial rule. As Stuart Hall writes, Babylon expresses "what Africa has *become* in the New World, what we have made of 'Africa': 'Africa' as we re-tell it through politics, memory and desire."[3] Such polyvalent symbols are crucial to the exploration of the new empire that is currently unfolding.

The Rastafari experience of Babylon, learnt over five centuries of slavery, colonialism and neo-colonialism, teaches us that to understand the empire, begin with the police. This optic on the new globalization would then merge with the way in which I have approached locality and the image via Rancière's theory of the subject and the police. American politics prior to 9-11 was dominated by a debate as to whether the country should serve as a "global policeman." As a candidate George W. Bush made much play with his opposition to such a stance. Subsequently, of course, the United States has declared that no region of the world is off-limits in its war against terrorism. As a global policeman, it has repeatedly instructed the rest of the world to "move on, there's nothing to see" (Rancière). The necessity of engaging that instruction is what constitutes a global politics today. At the same time, in the current climate of secrecy, few neutral or government sources are available to researchers. However, it is precisely because the print and visual media are the place in which people experience globalization that I am willing to take the risk of making a case against the global police based to some degree on materials drawn from the media. No doubt some emphases will come to seem misplaced or misinformed. To negotiate this unpredictability, I have sought to place the emergence of the global police into a long historical framework, based on a revision of Michel Foucault's theory of the disciplinary prison within a global context.

In this view, what has happened in the past decade is a shift within a 200-year-old debate in Western modernity about the boundaries between the national and the foreign, articulated in terms of race, gender and sexuality. In Foucault's famous analysis, the disciplinary reforming prison provided the key model for power in Western modernity.[4] I want to revise this model in two regards. First, I shall suggest that, if that disciplinary power is considered in the full context of slavery and colonialism that generated and supported it, it will come to be understood as always contested by, and in conflict with, the practices of deportation and spectacular punishment that Foucault claimed it had replaced. Second, in the shorter frame since the fall of communism after the revolutions of 1989, power has reverted from discipline to detention as a means of correction, entailing a shift in its model institution from the prison to the camp for migrants and refugees. This shift was enacted as a response to the sense that the combined effects of digital technology and globalization were eroding the basis of the nation state itself, the agent of disciplinary power. Even as the digital boom was beginning in the 1990s, the Anglophone governments of Australia, Britain and the United States changed their policies on imprisonment and asylum, abandoning the goals of reform, rehabilitation and refuge in favor of a strategy that can be called detain-and-deport. The camp for refugees and migrants has become the key institution of this strategy, a social model for our time that is the equivalent of the panopticon, Jeremy Bentham's ideal prison. The aim is to reassert the nation state as the key institution in enabling the free flow of capital while preventing the free movement of individuals that might threaten the continued viability of cheap labor markets.

It was, as it happened, precisely these countries that formed the active core of the coalition that attacked Iraq. The unlikely marriage of a very conservative Republican administration with the self-declared Third Way of Blair's New Labour and the isolationist Australian coalition led by John Howard was in part enabled because it articulated the new domestic detention regime as foreign policy, or even a global philosophy, centered on the power of the state. The domestic philosophy of pre-emptive punishment argues that if there is a possibility that a crime might be committed, it ought to be pre-empted by government action. Domestic pre-emption renders the borders that are now invisible to global capital into barriers for the global workforce, whether the invisible barriers of visas and passports, or the physical barriers being built by the US at its Mexico border and by Israel in the Occupied Territories. As a globalized foreign policy, it transforms the post-Second World War consensus, incarnated in the United Nations, that states should only intervene within other nation states with the evidence beyond a reasonable doubt required in criminal cases, into a judgment on the basis of probabilities, as if in a civil law suit. This extension of civil law and domestic policy to the international situation was at first a defensive response to the apparent reduction in importance of the nation state after the collapse of Soviet-style socialism in 1989–1991, but it has now taken on an aggressive new life of its own. It follows the logic of seeing the global as a network of localities and has generated a new approach to the network itself, which requires a careful supervision of the flows of digital culture. While much of this thinking stems from the radical right, it has used troubling questions, such as the failure to prevent genocide in Rwanda, to gain the adherence of significant sectors of American liberalism, as represented by Thomas Friedman of the *New York Times*, and has claimed some key figures from the left such as Christopher Hitchens.

It is now clear that globalization cannot be understood within the framework of the advanced capitalist societies alone. As Manuel Castells has argued, this ignores such questions as the importance of the collapse of the Soviet system and the new crises of immigration.[5] These dramas have created what Antonio Negri and Michael Hardt have called a "plural multitude of productive, creative subjectivities . . . They are in perpetual motion and they form constellations of singularities and events that impose continual global configurations on the system."[6] Estimates of the current numbers of migrants and refugees vary from 20 million to 100 million people, while far more have become legal migrants or live as expatriates. It was, as Achille Mbembe has noticed, precisely to enable "the management of the multitudes" that camps for refugees, migrants and asylum seekers have been integrated into empire.[7] The technology of the camp has evolved over the course of the twentieth century but it is now being adapted to the changed circumstances of globalization. Immigration law, with its summary justice and strong deference to executive power, has therefore become the basis for actions against terrorism.[8] These new detention camps are not extermination camps. Far from claiming a final solution, such a camp puts the very idea of a solution into abeyance, keeping its inmates invisible with the goal of having them forgotten. The all-encompassing justification that is now being offered for these pre-emptive domestic and international changes is the fight against international terrorism. I shall argue that this theory of pre-emption entails both a retrospective rewriting of recent history and, in its rhetoric of the "clash of civilizations" (see Section 2), a reimagination of global modernity.

In the rhetoric of civilizational conflict, it is not hard to hear the echo of the culture wars that dominated American domestic politics in the 1990s. This section suggests that the groundwork that enabled the emergence of the pre-emptive war and the empire of camps can be seen in the cultural debates prompted by the Internet and its apparent transformation of Western culture and economy in the period that culminated with the US 2002 election. Even as some sections of the digerati – as the proponents of a digital future were known – were imagining a networked global society of free-flowing movement, Western nation states were preparing to make such movement impossible. This conflict of ideals was not clearly defined over a specific issue but can be traced, as we shall see below, in the representation of the Internet as a world without borders, whether political or social, that then came to be reconfigured as a place out of control after the dotcom crash. In short, the global network society that appeared to be forming in the 1990s has now been challenged by what I shall call closed-circuit culture. This spectre was always present in the dystopian vision of the digital future offered by science fiction writers like William Gibson. In his classic 1984 novel *Neuromancer*, Gibson imagined a ruined post-industrial world from which the only escapes were the digital world of cyberspace – a term he coined in the book – and the orbiting space station called the Zion

Cluster, a Rastafari community. By placing the Rastas in space, Gibson suggests that digital and information society is the modern Babylon. The closed-circuit culture that has now emerged is a re-engineered return to what Paul Edwards has called "the closed world" of Cold War America. Edwards defines the closed world as a metaphor he borrows from theater, suggesting an artificial enclosed environment that is nonetheless "radically divided against itself."[9] So the contained global system of the Cold War marked by real barriers like the Berlin Wall or the Demilitarized Zone between the two Koreas, as well as metaphorical divides like the Iron Curtain, was also divided in its all-embracing struggle (as the foreign policy theorists had it) between capitalism and communism. In this view, culture becomes understood as system "constituted in and through metaphors, technologies and practices. The metaphors are information, communication, and program; the technologies are computation and control; and the practices are abstraction, simulation, engineering, and panoptic management."[10] Consequently, the return to a closed system has been marked most noticeably in the areas of digital technology and panoptic discipline. In this section, the move towards a closed system is mapped in the virtual sphere of the Internet, even as it has had very real consequences for people in time and space. It is important to emphasize this broader context, rather than accept that the Iraq war was solely tied to the events of 9-11, a connection that even George W. Bush has now had to admit to be chimerical. The terrorist attacks of 9-11 simply confirmed and enhanced the scope of this change. Note that the Australian government symbolically refused entry to the MV *Tampa*, carrying a shipload of refugees, in August 2001, knowing full well that this action was in contravention of the entire panoply of post-Second World War human rights and refugee legislation. The World Trade Center attacks provided the perfect retrospective justification for a decision that had been arrived at over a decade of cultural conflict.

Rethinking the panopticon

In building this argument, the interpretation of globalization after the invasion of Iraq therefore needs to begin with the crisis that engendered the modern disciplinary system in the last decades of the eighteenth century. Britain found itself unable to decide how to deal with a surge in its prison population that had prisoners piled up in rotting ships in British ports. Two solutions were proposed and enacted to varying degrees, with one gaining ascendancy over the other only to fall back later. The first was the deportation of criminals to the new colony of Australia that became the first experimental penal colony in modern history. Deportation holds that those who are not part of the nation must simply be kept out or expelled. The other option, strongly pressed by the Utilitarian Jeremy Bentham, was the reforming prison, which he called the panopticon. Bentham copied his design from one he had witnessed in his brother's factory in Russia. Russia was a serf-owning economy, a form of slavery in which the person is tied to land as chattel in the same fashion as buildings or animals. But Russian serfdom was also disciplinary, in the modern sense, rather than relying on spectacular punishment. Capital punishment was withdrawn for common law offences in 1753 in favor of prison sentences, followed by internal exile to the new colony of Siberia, a fact that did not escape the attention of nineteenth-century prison reformers.[11] An owner who wanted to punish his serf would send the individual to the police with a note detailing the punishment desired.[12] Unlike US and Caribbean plantation slavery, serfdom thus fully incorporated the apparatus of the state into its system of punishment. Bentham's purpose was to persuade the British government to adopt his system of moral discipline that brought together the moral discipline of the Jesuit colonies in Paraguay and the state-sanctioned punishment of the serf economy.

Characterized above all by constant surveillance of the inmates, the reforming prison was a form of factory, which Bentham described as "a mill for grinding rogues honest, and idle men industrious."[13] It took in criminals, prostitutes and other delinquents and turned them into respectable citizens. The sentence was a just measure of how long this reformation might take, as well as being a punishment. This prison system was based on the faith that everyone could contribute usefully to society if helped to do so. Bentham envisaged the widest social benefits from his system: "Morals reformed, health preserved, industry invigorated, instruction diffused, public burthens lightened, economy seated as it were upon a rock, the gordion knot of the poor laws not cut but untied – all by a simple idea in architecture."[14] Foucault used Bentham's panopticon as his model for the society of surveillance created in the West in the century after 1750. The panopticon was an inspection house for the reformation of morals, whether of prisoners, workers or prostitutes by means of constant surveillance that the inmates could not perceive, a system summed up by Foucault in the aphorism "visibility is a trap."[15] Foucault's insight has enabled a new understanding of the modern period as a series of linked endeavors to control and discipline people into what he called "docile bodies." This visibility changed the prisoner because he or she is aware of being watched, without being able to see the watcher. Knowing that they cannot escape this surveillance, prisoners actively decide to change their behavior. So what matters is not just that they are being watched but that they know they are being watched. That is, the visibility of the prison provided for an exchange of information from the prison authorities to the prisoner, which the latter then processed. Bentham was consistently careful to emphasize that only sane people should be incarcerated in his prison house for precisely this reason and modern incarceration has similarly been concerned to exclude the insane and others like minors held to be incapable of the use of reason. Visibility, then, transmits information that is rationally processed.

Bentham's system has a direct connection to the formation of Rastafari. As part of the process of the abolition of slavery in Jamaica, the British government set about reforming prisons and punishment in the island. One of the most cogent arguments of the abolitionists was the casual abuse of power by slave-owners in inflicting arbitrary and excessive punishment on the enslaved. A key measure of post-abolition government was the introduction of the treadmill into Jamaican prisons. The treadmill was a hollow wood cylinder fitted with steps. Prisoners had their hands tied to a bar above the treadmill and were forced to rotate the cylinder by continuously taking steps. This enforcement of discipline, as pointless and soul-destroying as military drill procedures, amounted in the telling phrase of the historian Thomas C. Holt to the "Jamaican panopticon."[16] Yet in the colonial "margins" the panopticon was far from fully effective, from the point of view of the authorities. In the Morant Bay uprising of 1865, according to historian Catherine Hall: "Months of tension between black people and white over land, labour and law erupted after an unpopular verdict from magistrates led to a demonstration and attempted arrests."[17] In the ensuing violence, eighteen officials and members of the militia were killed, leading to Governor Edward John Eyre calling out troops. More than 400 people were executed, another 600 flogged and 1000 homes were destroyed. Governor Eyre, who had learned his trade in Australia, received the support of numerous British intellectuals, such as Charles Dickens, Alfred, Lord Tennyson and John Ruskin, and Britain resumed direct rule of the colony. With the support of most white settlers, Eyre wrote to the Colonial Office: "What we want mainly are a strong government, an organized detective Police Force, and an extensive white colonization of our interior lands."[18] So colonial settlement, the police and a "strong government" were linked in both the minds of the white planters and the rebels. James McLaren, a colleague of the rebel leader Paul Bogle, argued their case effectively at a Baptist meeting: "I am still a slave by working from days to days." He was paid 2s. 6d. for a day's work in 1865, less than the 3s. 6d. budgeted by the government to feed prisoners in 1837. "But the white people say we are lazy and won't work."[19] The rebellion of 1865 and the violence it elicited were recalled over and again in Rastafari and help account for the fact that "Babylon" can mean either the entire colonial system in general or the police in particular. In effect, there was no difference for the African diaspora population of Jamaica.

So the panoptic prison was in reality far from being the perfect machine it has been claimed to be, whether at home or abroad, in which "permanent visibility ensures the automatic functioning of power."[20] In practice, the prison house was always contested by deportation, and always a technological failure. Even the question of permanent visibility, so central to the scheme, could not easily be solved in practice. Bentham at first proposed that the prisoners would be, in effect, backlit by large glass windows, while lamps backed by reflectors would continue visibility at night. On hearing the plan, Lord Westmoreland, Lord Lieutenant of Ireland simply said: "They will all get out." Bentham added bars to the windows and proposed that the new structure be built entirely of iron and glass, like the later Crystal Palace: "It will be a lantern, it will be a bee-hive; it will be a glass bee-hive; and a bee-hive without a drone."[21] But it was obvious that the need for security diminished the possibilities of perfect illumination and in his 1811 version of the scheme, Bentham proposed gaslight as a solution. Like his glass and iron structure, this idea was ahead of its time. Friedrich Albert Winsor, a German expatriate, installed gaslight in a public house in the Passage des Panoramas, Paris, in 1816 but it failed – gaslight was not widely installed until the 1830s.[22] When the British instead opted for penal deportation to the new colony of Australia, creating what has been called a "gulag continent,"[23] Bentham first tried to denounce the enterprise in a book-length pamphlet called *The Panopticon versus New South Wales*. When that failed, he then tried to assert that panopticons should be built in Australia anyway. The prison at Port Arthur, Van Diemen's Land (now Tasmania) for the most recalcitrant convicts did in fact come close to his specifications. But for the most part, once in Australia, convicts were expected to labor for the government to atone for their crimes. Rather than an exchange of information between the prison and the prisoner, the penal colony bartered freedom for work. The ultimate goal of the convict was to become an emancipist, a legal category that allowed the status of felon to be set aside for that of citizen, albeit under permanent threat of withdrawal for any breach of the law.

In Australia, because emancipation had been the goal for the white convicts, it was by extension impossible for the indigenous population. In 1860 the Board for the Protection of Aboriginals created internment camps for Aboriginals living in the country in order to separate the category of the native from that of the citizen.[24] Aboriginals of different peoples and language groups were herded together behind cattle fences in order to quietly die out. Such camps and other internment systems for the indigenous, the enslaved and the displaced, combined with the threat of deportation for domestic criminals, were always a counterpoint within the system of global discipline created by panoptic modernity. The deportation system argues by contrast that there is no such thing as society but only people who belong to the nation and those who do not. Deviant conduct indicated that people do not belong and that they should be expelled. As Angela Davis has argued, a full account of this counterpoint in the United States alone would require an examination of plantation slavery, Indian reservations, the Mission system and the internment camps for aliens created during both world wars. The deportation option was strongly promoted by conservative and radical thinkers alike. In his fierce critique of what he scornfully termed the "model prison," the celebrated Victorian historian and critic Thomas Carlyle considered that "the Devil's regiments of the line" were not to be dealt with domestically. A proper prison governor "will sweep them pretty rapidly into some Norfolk Island, into some special Convict Colony or remote domestic Moorland, into some stone-walled Silent System."[25] Nor was this simply rhetoric. Carlyle was part of a defense committee that ensured that Governor Eyre suffered no penalty for the spectacular violence he used in suppressing the Morant Bay rebellion of 1865. Although Britain stopped sending convicts to Australia in 1868, pro-deportation sentiments did not disappear. In 1896, the Reverend Osbourne Jay, a reforming and progressive cleric in Bethnal Green at the heart of London's East End, declared in an interview that the only solution to the problem of the poor was "to stop the supply of persons born to be lazy, immoral and deficient. This can only be done by sending the present stock of them to what I will call a penal settlement."[26] Jay's view was influenced by Francis Galton's theory of eugenics, which held that humans needed to be bred for moral qualities, just as livestock were bred for physical ones. By removing those determined to be deviant or unfit from the "lifestream," society could eliminate its problems.

So while Bentham believed that the panopticon would reform deviance out of a society, the opposing view saw offenders as incorrigible defects. The only option was to remove them by deportation or by otherwise preventing them from reproducing within the mother country. To this end many American states legalized the sterilization of prisoners and mental patients in the early twentieth century. Eugenics and the penal colony in its various forms were not an exception but the constant counterpoint to the reforming prison, deployed with great energy throughout the twentieth century. Many worry that the current advances in genetics may allow a revival of such ideas. For despite the growth of the prison in Victorian Britain, Bentham was unsuccessful in persuading governments to adopt his scheme in detail. He opposed the imposition of silence on prisoners, one of the key features of the Victorian prison endorsed by Carlyle in his critique of "model" Benthamite prisons. Bentham saw silence as unleashing imagination rather than reason, his agent of reform:

> When the external senses are restrained from action, the imagination is more active, and produces a numerous race of ideal beings. In a state of solitude, infantine superstitions, ghosts, and specters, recur to the imagination. This, of itself, forms a sufficient reason for not prolonging this species of punishment, which may overthrow the powers of the mind, and produce incurable melancholy.[27]

As time went by, Bentham came to despair of the panopticon. Writing of his papers on the subject, he declared: "It is like opening a drawer where devils are locked up – it is breaking into a haunted house."[28]

The panopticon was supposed to make its inmates reflect on their crimes and submit to discipline in perfect visibility. The dark, silent prisons that were actually built in the nineteenth century created only ghosts. Nonetheless, in its heyday the hybrid "panoptic" prison appeared to be a success from the official point of view. To pursue the British example, by 1877 the number of prisons in Britain was only 56, down from 113 in Bentham's day. Prison reform initiated in 1898 moved the penitentiary system closer to the moralizing machine Bentham had imagined, abolishing the silent rule, while retaining certain punitive elements. After 1918 a further 29 prisons were closed and by 1952 the total number of prisons in the UK was 29. In 1992, the prison population in Britain was 40,600, down from 51,000 in 1988. In the subsequent decade the number of prisoners rose by 50 percent and now totals 72,000, even though crime rates are falling. This total is anticipated to hit 92,000 in 2005,[29] but with current legal reforms making it harder to present a viable defense in many cases, this may well be an underestimate.

Detain and deport: after panopticism

As if to announce that the 200-year-old experiment with the reforming prison was over, Britain has recently returned to the eighteenth-century strategy of using prison ships. With HMP *Weare* moored in Portland Harbour, Dorset, without controversy, government plans now call for a second such ship in Scotland. The prison population in the United States, where over two million people are now incarcerated in the penal system, dwarfs such numbers. Led by a political reaction epitomized in the "three strikes and you're out" laws, prisoner numbers have escalated to previously unthinkable levels. These laws consign any person convicted of three felonies to prison for life on the belief that more crime will thus be prevented because the perpetrator is clearly an incorrigible recidivist. By the end of 2002, the total number of Americans in prison exceeded two million for the first time for a total of 2,166,620. Broken down into states and ethnicities, this raw figure, shocking as it is, conceals a remarkable racist divide. At the time of calculation, 12 percent of black men aged 20 to 34 were in prison, compared to 1.6 percent of whites, according to the Justice Department. Louisiana, with a significant African American population, had 799 inmates per 100,000 of population, compared to 137 in all but entirely white Maine. Even the federal government now admits that 28 percent of black men will be imprisoned at some point in their lives.[30] Global capital has abandoned any belief in the reforming character of incarceration in favor of a simple and profitable strategy of pre-emptive mass detention. The contemporary American system is not, then, one of "corrections," despite the continuing use of this term, but one of detention.

In Australia, Britain and the United States, the change to a detain-and-deport system preceded 9-11 by almost a decade. This conservative policy on prisons was enacted by both liberal and conservative administrations alike as part of the "triangulation" between the poles of political opinion that was held to be the key to political success in the period. In this view, liberals and leftists adopted a tough penal policy as the price of becoming electable, just as conservatism needed to present a compassionate face. But the mistake being made by the liberal left was strategic, rather than tactical. For just as Western nations consolidated this domestic return to what Mrs. Thatcher had famously called Victorian values, there was also a shift in neo-conservative Western foreign policy, following the Huntington thesis that history was going to become the site of a "clash of civilizations" between the supposedly Christian West and Islam. With the ascendancy of this faction in George W. Bush's administration, the detain-and-deport carceral philosophy has become a key tool in the clash of civilizations and vice versa. Pre-empting terrorism is to win the war of civilizations, while diluting national culture with overseas immigrants, especially Muslims, is to lose it. As we know, this strategy of pre-emption has now become the national security policy of the United States. In a brief 30-page essay replete with standard clichés, the Bush administration has radically redirected American power towards pre-emption of attack. Pre-emption is a curious word. It might be glossed as being a revision of the former policy of prevention by the unfailing belief of the fundamentalist right in their own redemption: pre-emption. Here, rather than prevent crime or war by rehabilitation or deterrence, you mobilize your unfailing belief in your own redemption to attack those you have determined to be your enemies before they can attack you. A corollary of this imagined community is the normally peaceful citizen, who "plays by the rules" to use one of Bill Clinton's most effective tags. Violence is a threat to this person that the state claims it will now prevent by offering itself as "tough on crime, tough on the causes of crime" (Tony Blair). While this formula was popular precisely because it suggested that crime has social causes, in practice the Blair government has concentrated on incarcerating its perpetrators, a philosophy that has become part of Western neo-liberal "common sense." This cure for crime was effectively envisaged by the film *Minority Report* (2002), based on a short story by Philip K. Dick. On the basis of what we might call a think-tank (a group of clairvoyants able to predict future crimes), the police in this film pre-empt crime by arresting its perpetrators before they act. Normality is sustained by preventing any disruption from the internal wild zones of the poor and the dispossessed.

The national and the digital in the 1990s

This shift towards exclusion and force as state policy was at odds with the rise of global digital capital in the late 1990s that briefly hinted at the redundancy of the nation state. In the 90s, a new global society seemed to be emerging in which digital technology was the most obvious indication of a new world without frontiers. Capital had gone global in the financial deregulation movement of the 1980s, with huge sums of money being moved around the world at the touch of a button. The French socialist administration elected in 1981 was the first to feel the bite of the newly empowered markets. Elected after decades in opposition, the new ministers had not reached their desks before foreign currency traders had created a run on the franc that immediately curtailed

their freedom of action. Far from being able to enact the redistributive policies on which it was elected, the new government
had to pursue market-friendly initiatives in order to prevent a
financial disaster. Even the American government was constrained
by the new markets as Bill Clinton learnt to his distaste after his
1992 election. Again, his gently redistributive policy was shelved
to keep the bond market happy. According to *Wired* magazine and
other digital boosters, like Nicholas Negroponte of the MIT Media
Lab, the 1990s were supposed to be the decade that consolidated
the network society as a place of freedom of movement for ideas
and people as well as capital.[31] Political and financial agreements
like the expansion of the European Union and the North Atlantic
Free Trade Agreement seemed to be moving in this direction. But
above all, the emergence of the Internet as what became known
as the Electronic Frontier seemed to be about to change the rules
of the nation state forever. At the height of the dotcom boom,
Silicon Valley was actually minority white, as a convergence of hi-
tech engineers from India and East Asia with Latina/o manual and
service labor pushed the "white" demographic into the minority.
These local facts were mere by-products, according to the new
digerati, of the emergence of the digital nomad. For social scien-
tist Arjun Appadurai, writing in 1993, it was clear that "[i]n the
postnational world we are seeing emerge, diaspora runs with, and
not against, the grain of identity, movement and reproduction."[32]
But increasingly the question has become whose diaspora is
being permitted and enabled by this moment of globalization.
Cyberprophet Jacques Attali claimed that a new class was emerging
that he called "liberated nomads bound by nothing but desire and
imagination, greed and ambition."[33] This new superclass, crossing
national boundaries at will, use their "nomadic objects" like WiFi
laptops, satellite phones and Global Positioning System direction
finders to enable their new liberty.

However, like all nomads, they depend on others staying put.
In this instance, global nomadism requires a workforce prepared
to relocate on a local or national level but not allowed to cross
national boundaries. This local use of force has been validated and

enabled by a resurgence in the traditional power of the nation state to hold a monopoly on extreme violence. The need for state-sponsored and controlled violence has long been the prime rationale for the nation state itself. This violence is then offered as a solution for random violence among the subject population. As Susan Buck-Morss has pointed out, the state imagines itself as requiring a "wild zone of power" in which the usual laws do not apply in order to sustain precisely those usual laws.[34] Rather than being an exception to the rule, this wild zone is the normal justification for the continued power of the state against radical arguments for the "withering away" of the state and conservative pleas to constantly diminish government alike. The permanent war that has been declared on "terrorism" has mandated the strongest resurgence of the nation state imaginable, dealing a significant blow to hopes for a global society. In this sense, what Giorgio Agamben has called the "state of exception" has increasingly become the norm, so that government has appropriated powers for itself that would have seemed inconceivable a few years ago.[35]

So digital culture attempted to imagine a newly fluid social arena at the same moment as Western nation states were reverting to a detain-and-deport model of jurisprudence as a means of self-validation. These two modes of social imaginary were intimately connected and the brief apparent tussle between them has for now been resolved in favor of the "hard" options: incarceration, immobility, and heterosexual masculinity. Global digital culture needed to create not so much the social and cultural conditions for the hybrid network society it desired, as "*the capacity to imagine them.*"[36] In retrospect, the failure to make this imaginary leap began at the level of the network itself. Most descriptions imagined the web as a perfectly rhizomatic form, unencumbered by the bottle-necks and intersections of "real" space because the network would, by definition, route data around any such hold-up. IBM engineers created a map of the Internet in January 2001 that showed a very different space. Looking at the links by which the network was created and is sustained, IBM found a "strongly connected" core of some 50 million nodes at the heart of the Internet, creating a bow-tie pattern. But just as many nodes were to be found, weakly connected or disconnected altogether, behind password-protected firewalls and intranets. As viruses and worms continue to disable hundreds of thousands of computers running Microsoft software, the company now officially recommends users to install firewalls, even on domestic computers. Spam means that email filters are mandatory for all users, while parents, schools and libraries install content filters on web browsers for fear of pornography. That suggests that the Internet, the grand metaphor for and expression of the network society, increasingly requires a series of border controls and checks, like the traditional nation state, rather than being the free-flowing dream-space of so much media imagining. If that is the case, there is a major task of reconceptualization at hand.

The new knowledge economy, or "soft capitalism," of the 1990s relied on a flow of practice that seemed to require new social agents. Out of the endless flows of available knowledge, an enterprise (or enterprising individual) had to abstract certain data to form information. With that information, a profit could be made either directly in the market or indirectly by calling the attention of others to that information. This "attention economy," as Jonathan L. Beller has called it, generated profit by catching people's attention, known in the digital world as first "capturing" and then "monetizing eyeballs."[37] These imaginary flows of information created a series of global opposites by which to give themselves contrast and depth that had very real effects. The dotcom economy tried to gender its agency as a form of what might be called flexible masculinity. Its failure of imagination enabled, and in some quarters mandated, the return of a vengeful masculinity. Within the attention economies of the advanced capitalist societies, a flexible male agency had to "go with the flow" and overcome "hysterical reactions to information technologies."[38] To be successful in the new business world, agency needed to be sufficiently masculine (not hysterically feminine) but flexible. This new masculinity was represented by the casual dress and grooming of the new elites that was institutionalized in the United States as "casual Friday," on which business suits were set aside for "casual" clothes. The paradigm for such agency was the day traders who sprang up in the mid-90s. There was no more typical phenomenon of the digital boom than the day trader, a person (usually a white man) buying and selling securities on-line on the same day, hoping to make a series of small profits out of the standard fluctuations of the market. Not only was this practice impossible prior to the expansion of securities firms onto the Internet, but also it contradicted one of the oldest axioms of investing that money should be invested over the long term. Here shares were bought and sold in minutes rather than years. It was a prime example of what was called "Internet time," the compression of time and space by digital technology. The flow of market knowledge was converted by the day trader into information on which he acted and profited. Failure was a failure of character as tested by the market. Opposed to the day trader was the caricature of the "welfare queen." Usually represented as an African American woman, the welfare queen in hegemonic political discourse ignored all opportunities presented by the information society in favor of dependency on welfare. By using the rhetoric of addiction, poverty and unemployment could be presented as moral flaws.

This gendered tension in the capitalist societies was reversed when the attention economy turned its head towards the developing world. Here the virtuous figure was the subaltern woman, who, as Gayatri Spivak has pointed out, is "now to a rather large extent the support of production,"[39] through piecework, sweatshop labor and reproductive labor in low-wage economies. The low-wage production of the global economy depends on these women remaining where they are so they can be underpaid. The demon figure of Western attention is, then, the migrant worker, figured as male. This person has been extensively denounced for migrating solely for economic reasons, as if this was a new and wild variant on immigration, rather than the primary motive of those the Statue of Liberty hails as the "poor and huddled masses." This reversal of gender roles was effected by the long-established gender roles of Orientalism. The "Oriental" man is, by definition, morally suspect and sexually deviant. "Oriental" women are split into the opposed figures of the sexual temptress in the harem and the oppressed victim of backward societies, metonymically represented by the veil. It was for this reason that such unlikely feminists as Laura Bush endorsed the war on Afghanistan as a liberation of women. One might even suggest that women freed from the veil were now available to work in "rebuilding" the economy. It is precisely because this cast of characters is imagined, rather than objectively real, and has a long history in Western culture, that it resists satire and statistics alike. With the apparent collapse of the knowledge/attention economy, refusing the migrant worker and the welfare queen became still more powerful tropes for a threatened domestic audience. Linked to terrorism, the revived imperialist/Orientalist narrative has, despite its obvious flaws and inconsistencies, given coherence to the invasion and occupation of Iraq.

The identity of globalization

It is worth recalling that globalizing the capitalist economy has always required drastic restrictions on individual rights and freedoms. The 1990s were often compared to the 1890s for their mutual sense of *fin-de-siècle*, their innovation and their global character. Indeed, by some measures, including the vital question of foreign direct investment (overseas investment into a domestic economy), the globalization of the present is still only roughly equal to that of the era of high imperialism that ended in 1914.[40] Yet this freedom of capital was enabled by a conjuncture of political strategies based on legislating difference as absolute rather than relative. Oscar Wilde's trial for gross indecency in 1895 has been understood by modern scholarship as establishing "the" homosexual as a separate species of human being.[41] It was followed in the United States by the Supreme Court's upholding of segregation in *Plessey* v. *Ferguson* in 1896, legalizing the division of the United States by blood, using the infamous "one drop of blood" laws that defined people as black – and hence legally inferior – if they had any African ancestry whatsoever.[42] The spread of virulent anti-Semitism around Europe following Emile Zola's 1898 denunciation of the abuse of state power in the Dreyfus Case turned the ancient religious prejudice into a biological and cultural separation between Aryan and Jew, whose consequences are all too well known. By 1900, the barriers of sexual and ethnic division for the modern period were in place. In 1903, W.E.B. Dubois reflected on this crisis and famously observed that the problem of the twentieth century would be the "color line." With that line reinforced and overlapped by the policing of (hetero)sexuality and of Aryanism, Dubois was even more right than he had feared.

Despite the evident extension of personal freedoms in the West since the 1960s, the current moment of globalization is similarly based on a reactionary redefinition of identity that, from the point of view of government, requires new modes of surveillance and internment. The line that is being drawn in this instance separates a sexualized definition of the "civilized" Christian citizen from the nomadic and barbaric Islamic migrant. The famous "flows" of globalization identified by Arjun Appadurai in 1990 have been dammed.[43] In the era of digital culture (1981–2000), free-flowing capital created free-flowing desires. At a certain moment, these desires started to cross the lines intended to contain them. Digital products started to want to be free, not just in the classic liberal sense of free markets, but free of charge and even politically free. At this point, national governments made a concerted effort to close the global circuit and to end the freedom of the so-called Napster era. Although a global networked society is still extremely difficult to regulate – as the continuing flow of file-sharing, whether of music or film, amply demonstrates – it is clear that the utopian moment of digital culture has passed. The extent to which this closure will be fully effective is yet to be determined and forms the underlying ground for much cultural and political activism.

If we look back to the 1990s moment of what seemed to be a constantly expanding US stock market on which the new order depended, one can see that globalization explicitly marketed itself as homosociality – a same-sex social world – with a distinctly homoerotic edge that was present but not named. Of course many women were and are successful in both fields but the culture remains overwhelmingly masculine. It still seems that the greater the speculative risk, the higher the number of men. While the New York Stock Exchange has at least a few women on the floor, the more risky Chicago Futures Market is astonishingly white and male for a modern institution. One index of the changing desires and fears that resulted in the digital marketplace of day traders was the striking television commercials for the new dotcom companies. Advertising was critical to the dotcom companies because it was their only form of interaction with the public capable of generating revenue. In a certain sense, the ad was the company, leading to a very high number of repeat showings. At the same time, by representing the new and unfamiliar world of the Internet in the known format of the television commercial, such advertising had the effect of creating a representational context for the virtual reality of the web. Certain advertisements seemed to embody the new ethos of the Internet as freedom. This moment began with Ridley Scott's famous commercial for Apple Computers, shown just once during the 1984 Superbowl. It depicted a young woman smashing a screen showing a Big Brother figure, paying homage to George Orwell's novel *1984*, even as it suggested that the computer was the means to liberation. By the 1990s MCI's "Anthem" campaign fleshed out this claim: "There is no race. There is no gender. There is no age. There are no infirmities. There are only minds. Utopia? No, Internet."[44] Difference itself could now be disposed of by reducing all differences to the zeroes and ones of the computer. This utopia prompted Microsoft to ask its users: "Where do you want to go today?" The implication was that there was no limit to one's choice but many hackers suspected the question was asked because Microsoft had no idea what to do with the Internet. If these enticing images and ideas seem to bear little relation to the day-to-day slog through email and corporate websites, that did nothing to diminish their allure as the imaginary of the Internet above and beyond what it had hitherto become. On-line you could be whoever you wished to be, as new media pundits endlessly reminded us. One reason for the demise of Britain's Conservative government in 1997 was that it seemed terminally out of touch with such developments, offering what sociologist Mary Evans has called "a subtext of terrified masculinity as well as the actual text of bluster and xenophobia."[45] It is a measure of the shift that has taken place in the past seven years that the once-derided Conservative world view is again dominant.

Controlling the flow

In 1997 a Clinton White House policy paper declared that:

> The US government supports the broadest possible free flow of information across national borders. This includes most informational material now accessible and transmitted through the Internet, including World Wide Web pages, news and other information services, virtual shopping malls and entertainment features.[46]

Needless to say, such policy is now firmly in the dustbin of history, prompted first by the dotcom crash and then by the rise of international anti-globalization violence. As early as 1998, the federal government had moved away from the fantasy of digital openness towards the concrete restrictions on digital property that have become the symbol of the end of that era. With the passing of the Digital Millennium Copyright Act (1998), a challenge was made to the radical software belief in "copyleft," the notion that the basic source code of any software should be available to everyone for free. The most notable successes of this movement have been the Apache software for servers and the alternative Linux operating system. Linux, however, has been adopted by IBM and Apple has begun to make its source codes available so that hackers can improve it for the company free of charge. For Matthew Arnison of Indymedia, "Free software is the main resistance against the privatization of the Internet."[47] While many consumers simply enjoyed the free products, the Copyright Act laid the ground for the music business to close down the Napster file-sharing service and to send out several thousand subpoenas in July 2003 to individuals using peer-to-peer file-sharing software like Morpheus and Kazaa. As the emphasis shifted, the fiber-optic connections offered by transnational cable companies like FLAG, the Fiberoptic Link Around the Globe, can be seen in a different light (see www.flag telecom.com). Now the longest man-made structure in existence, far exceeding the Great Wall of China, FLAG retains the ownership of its cable at all times, only renting their use to other companies. In this way it is positioned to control what content does or does not become available to users. In 1998 this would have seemed like a paranoid fantasy. By 2003, the Chinese government had shut down some 150,000 Internet cafés, while in Singapore all Internet connections have to be made through the closely monitored government provider Signet, and in America, the USA Patriot Act (2001) gives the government access to all email and other digital information without prior warrant.

The closing down of the net was figured as a restoration of appropriate gender identity after the fluid perversion of the dotcom era. When the NASDAQ tanked in April 2000, a post on the day trader bulletin boards operated by the digital boom television station CNBC from a man claiming to have been involved in the battle against the 1968 Tet offensive launched by the North Vietnamese army in South Vietnam, highlighted the issue: "Someday you will comprehend the difference between real danger and hysteria." From his point of view, those panicking were "clearly raised in a family without a male, only female raised children act like you."[48] In this condensed invective, real men were bred in traditional nuclear families and brought to maturity by fighting in imperialist wars. By contrast, feminine men, the old euphemism for queers, were responsible for the market's loss of nerve. Real men continued to trade as bulls. This behavior was encouraged by CNBC itself who were even talking up "opportunities" throughout the week of April 7–14, 2000 when the NASDAQ prices dropped by over 25 percent. As the screen swirled with a web-like mass of data on stock prices and market trends, the word "opportunity" was marked out in stable, bold form. In response to the Tet post, one trader claimed that: "First they hated the blacks and Native Americans and women, and now they include anybody in their 20s who has made money."[49] The neoliberal theory of man (gender intended) that so dominated global political and cultural life was spinning out of control.[50] Was the trader a hypermasculine soldier or an oppressed minority? Did he desire the infantile pleasures of flowing money or the stern discipline of the Protestant nuclear family? Traders suddenly discovered that the little hand on their web-browser that hovered over the "order" button was not the invisible hand of the market-place, but was just stroking their leg.

The paradox of the global economy of the period was that it entirely depended on the homosociality of the men that dominate trading, especially on-line, but perceived any unconventional masculinity, let alone overt homosexuality, as the collapse of the market. Like the purloined letter in Edgar Allan Poe's short story of the same name, the desired and disavowed object was in full view in the trading room. But its compulsory visuality depends on a compulsory heterosexuality with which it is in flagrant contra-diction. The closeted, embedded heterostructures (to borrow a term from laser technology) of global capital were not capable of sustaining an overlap with panoptical discipline. For at the heart of the machine is a paradox. The panopticon relied on a rational interpretation of visualized information by the object of its disci-pline for it to function properly. Yet as Freud remarked many years ago, the "ego is not master in its own house." The implica-tion was that the ego is analogous to the stern Victorian father whose patriarchal rule was always under challenge even within his own house. Oscar Wilde had maintained a double life as a husband and father as well as his "feasting with panthers" in closeted queer culture. When he failed to keep those worlds sufficiently distinct he was prosecuted, imprisoned and later exiled. In rather similar fashion, day trading, like the extended dotcom boom of which it was a prominent symptom, simply could not sustain the intense contradictions of sexual, gender and national identity required to keep the market fantasy alive. In order to restore the markets – from the point of view of capital – a restoration of these threatened and interlinked modes of identity was required and has been enacted.

The entire edifice of the 90s boom was constructed on the irrational belief that market prices are rational responses to economic realities, the so-called "rational choice" theory. As shares continued to rise, the bull market media insisted that a new business cycle had dawned, enabled by the productivity of the computer and the new marketplace created by the Internet. All the pieces depended on each other, as in a house of cards. If the Internet was a new engine of profit, then it made sense to invest in Internet-oriented businesses and it made equal sense to do so online. In the crash, the market was suddenly held to be revealed as a hysterical, feminine space. Richard D. Rippe, chief economist at Prudential Securities asserted that: "Markets move on emotion." Business guru Knight Kiplinger similarly explicated the Asian financial crisis in language that blended sadomasochism with imperialism: "As the nations of Asia discovered in 1997–98, foreign capital is a stern master."[51] Here capital was represented as masculine to Asia's feminine; more specifically, capital is the dominant to Asia's submissive. Indeed, American and European firms acquired $12 billion worth of Asian businesses in the first half of 1998, displacing the 38 percent of investments in Asia formerly held by developing nations.[52] Thus, when capital punished the Asian nations it did so rationally, but when it bit the master's hand in the United States, it became feminized as emotive.

Traders were now represented not as rational theoreticians of the market but as hysterics: "They were nervous coming into the trading day and traders seized on [the rise of] the CPI [Consumer Price Index] as justification for continuing to be bearish."[53] Traders were seen as acting on their nervousness, rather than on rational market information. In an essay looking back at the boom as the crash unfolded, the New York Times scolded those who had boosted the stocks of companies such as iVillage, a site cluster for women. iVillage's shares had risen from an offering price of $24 to a first day close over $80 in March 1999. A year later the *Times* agonized: "How could a rational market push the share prices of these nascent companies to such heights?"[54] On the cyberrebel site Net Slaves, iVillage was equally critiqued: "iVillage is my personal whipping boy because they have committed a multitude of sins. First and foremost, they ran through a 100 million US dollars. You could buy a small country for that. You could live a hundred lifetimes with that kind of cash."[55] Note again the explicitly sadomasochist and imperialist language in discussing a site that was organized by, and marketed to, women. Rational market decisions could no longer be entrusted to the dispersed and decentered digital culture. The presumption that the trader visualized by the global digital panopticon would behave in a rational manner now seemed unsustainable. The solution was that always predicated by the disciplinary system and already being enacted at the national level in terms of penal policy: revert to a detain-and-deport nation state and use the newly configured "hi-tech Orientalism" to justify it.[56]

Building the empire of camps

One of the first nations to implement this policy was Australia, long haunted by the fear of Asia. Since 1992, everyone seeking asylum or refugee status in Australia has been sent to remote refugee camps, which have been convincingly linked to the nineteenth-century camps for Aboriginals. The new internment camps are not reforming institutions but simply serve as detention centers. Australia's notorious "White Australia" policy had been implemented after Federation by means of the *Immigration Restriction Act* (1901), in order to keep Asian workers out of the country. The neo-conservative administration led by John Howard saw an opportunity to revive its fortunes by reverting to a state-led hostility to immigrants. In August 2001, Howard refused the MV *Tampa* permission to dock on the Australian territory of

Christmas Island because the vessel was carrying several hundred refugees rescued from a sinking boat. While Howard anticipated the ensuing controversy, he could not have known that the events of September 11, 2001 were about to hand him a blanket endorsement of detain-and-deport Orientalism. It did not matter that most of the refugees affected were Afghanis and Iraqis fleeing the very regimes that Australia has since gone to war to overthrow. All were subsumed as Orientals, and hence the object of rejection, by being named "sleepers for terrorism," a charge that proved as effective as it was impossible to refute. Emboldened by the popular support for their stance, the Australian government has now implemented what it calls a "Pacific solution" by refusing to bring refugees to mainland Australia at all. Instead refugees are kept in camps on small Australian islands or, preferably, in other Pacific nations while awaiting an almost interminable "processing." Howard literally bribed the financially strapped government of the small Pacific island of Nauru to accept such asylum seekers by flying out a suitcase full of cash for their use in late 2001.

Those refugees who do make it to Australia, or who were already there, are being interned in remote camps. The low structures of the camps do nothing to draw attention to themselves and have no central viewpoint or command post. They are located in remote areas, such as the Woomera camp in South Australia, situated some 300 miles from the nearest town, Adelaide, on a vast rocket-testing site, once used by the US Army and still in service today. Their location is meant to emphasize that they are not part of the nation state and that their inmates will not achieve asylum, let alone citizenship. In this way the relics of the Cold War closed system have become components for the new global closed circuit culture, exemplified by the extraordinary US detention center at Guantánamo Bay, Cuba. Its first incarnation was appropriately named Camp X-Ray, a place beyond normal vision, in which mere flesh cannot be seen. Now most prisoners are incarcerated in the blandly named Camp Delta, living in cells eight feet by seven feet with only three twenty-minute periods for exercise a week. Unsurprisingly, detainees made 24 suicide attempts in the first two years of the camp's operation, a problem common to all the detain-and-deport centers. Woomera is presently surrounded with fences and coils of razor wire that will soon be replaced with an electrified fence, delivering a "non-fatal electronic shock" to anyone trying to escape. As such construction goes ahead it becomes clear that the camps are intended not as a temporary response to an imagined crisis but as permanent features of the legal system. They mark a radical reversal of state policy to foreigners, or, as the United States likes to call them, aliens.

These camps are not the exception to democratic society. Rather they are the exemplary institution of a system of global capitalism that supports the West in its high consumption, low-price consumer lifestyle. I call this regime the empire of camps. Conservative thinkers in the United States have become surprisingly comfortable with the term "empire" as a response to 9-11 and new books on the subject are published almost every week. George Bush has compared the occupation of Iraq to that of the Philippines in 1898, an avowedly civilizing mission of the old school – and one also promoted by inaccurate "intelligence." My use of the term "empire" was at first appropriated from Michael Hardt and Antonio Negri's instant classic *Empire* (2000) that analyses the new geo-politics of globalization. But Hardt and Negri's vision of a decentered empire has come to be overtaken by the assertion of a more familiar model of empire controlled by a particular nation state. Drawing on the work of Claude Nicolet, a historian of the Roman Empire, Irit Rogoff has defined empire as "the spatialization of a concept which is played out through the evolution of technologies of mobility and surveillance and through a consciousness of boundaries that expand far beyond the self."[57] While empire has a wide range of meanings, this definition is very pertinent to the empire of camps. The camps in question are the internment camps for migrants and refugees that are the symbol of the new world order. Critics from Giorgio Agamben to Angela Davis and Paul Gilroy have understood the camp as a key index of modernity. Agamben, for example, writes that "the birth of the camp in our time appears as an event that decisively signals the political space of modernity itself."[58] The refugee camp marks a new twist in that modernity, for while they are, of course, very similar to detention and concentration camps of earlier periods (if not to the extermination camps of the Nazis), it is important to register that they are also something new.

The camp is the panopticon for our time, at once the site of deployment of new visual technologies, a model institution for global culture and a powerful symbol of the renewed desire of nation states to restrict global freedom of movement to capital and deny it to people. To this end, the empire has used a degree of force that would have been unthinkable without the enabling context of September 11. For all its religious overtones, the empire of camps has no scruples, no moral agenda and no desire to be seen or to make its prisoners visible, although surveillance is everywhere. The grand architectural sweep of the panoptic prison, the department store and the military barracks, has been replaced by the low-rise internment camp, the strip mall and the anonymous delivery of "smart" weapons. In an important example, US high schools now operate behind metal detectors and with closed-circuit TV surveillance, unable to rely on traditional discipline. In one extraordinary case, high school pupils in private Jesuit colleges funded by the Bill and Melinda Gates Foundation are sent to work for businesses for five days a month without recompense. The school receives funds for their labor that are used to support operating costs.[59] The *maquilladora* factories turning out cheap products for the US economy on the Mexican side of the border are another key example of this low-wage high-surveillance economy. While the department store and the Arcade were the commercial outlets of panopticism, the camp retails via the strip mall, the outlet store and the suburban superstore. Here appearances are sacrificed to the cash nexus: you get the steak cheaply but you have to supply the sizzle yourself, as we saw in the discussion of Wal-Mart in Section 2.

Now the empire of camps has further challenged what seemed to many, in the first stages of this era of globalization, to be the revenge of the nomads by reclassifying the nomad as a person fully incapable of being emancipated into citizenship. As such the detainees are kept in a realm of the undead, under total observation but out of sight. This politics of ghostly subjection requires a re-emancipation of time and space. Detainees, even children, are given nothing to do and have no information as to what may happen to them. Nothing could be further from the rational exchange of information that structured the panopticon. Arguably, the Orientalist theory behind the camps denies rationality to the inmates in any event, reinforced by the Western theory that Islam and the terrorism it is supposed to engender are anti-rational belief systems. For whereas the panoptic institution at least aspired to reform their inmates, the camps are specifically intended to generate, in the words of the Australian government's own human rights advisory group, "a miasma of despair and desperation."[60] Inmates are then offered deportation with a small cash incentive in the belief that they will feel anything to be better than their detention. In 2003, the British government proposed taking children of refugees who refuse to leave into care as hostages to ensure their parents' departure, prompting protests even from the Conservative opposition.

As Alison Bashford and Carolyn Strange have argued, these camps owe as much in inspiration to quarantine procedures as they do to prisons as such. Building on legislation passed in 1908 that gave the Australian government extensive powers of detention, a system of quarantine was established that maintained leper colonies on remote islands as recently as the 1960s.[61] The rhetoric of hygiene that motivated quarantine procedures was also a key part of the rationale of eugenics that sought to breed "imperfections" out of society, by force if necessary. These insistent and circular implications – prison implies quarantine which implies eugenics which implies internment camps – form the logic of the detain-and-deport model of social order. Foucault saw quarantine as one model for the disciplinary society, based on measures to control outbreaks of social and medical disorder: "Behind the disciplinary mechanisms can be read the haunting memory of 'contagions,' of the plague, of rebellions, crimes, vagabondage, desertions, people who appear and disappear, love and die in disorder."[62] Quarantine, then, is always as much a means of social control as it is a medical matter. These procedures are still very much part of the present.

It is instructive to see how the SARS outbreak, concurrent with the war in Iraq, was quickly brought to heel by quarantine procedures in China, Hong Kong and Toronto, the leading sites of infection, while the anthrax attacks of 2001 remain a mystery. For the biological weapon anthrax was delivered in modern fashion by mail, whereas the SARS virus, although clearly spread by air travel, could be contained in very traditional manner by incarcerating the sick. At the same time, the Bush administration is claiming credit for promoting initiatives against AIDS in Africa, even though it has requested only two-thirds of the relevant budget item. In an exclusionary model of discipline, quarantine and disease control are paradigmatic, not the reforming prison.

In Australia, the camps have been met with principled and courageous protests, such as a series of wire-cutting protests at Woomera that allowed inmates a temporary freedom. Echoing the Australian Freedom Buses of the 1960s that culminated with the granting of citizenship to Aboriginal peoples for the first time in 1967, the Imaginepeace Busketeers attacked the fences of the camps, flew kites over the wire, or passed flowers and messages over the dividing line between the alien and the citizen. Unlike in the 1960s, governments welcome such protests as an opportunity to demonstrate their determination and rigor. When a family facing deportation from Britain in 2002 sought refuge in a mosque, the police had no compunction in breaking down the door to drag them out. The imprisoned refugees in Woomera and in the British camp of Yarl's Wood have resorted to burning down their huts in protest. Built at cost of £100 million, Yarl's Wood was opened in January 2002 to house over 1000 asylum seekers. Home Secretary David Blunkett hoped to deport over 2500 people a month from Yarl's Wood and contracted the center out to the private Group 4 Security firm. Their conduct was so poor that even a government prosecutor later referred to them as a "national laughing stock." The first riot was provoked as early as February

2002, when Younis Igwegbe, a Nigerian woman, was prevented from going to chapel on a Sunday. Other inmates took her side and things escalated to the point where the entire center was burned to the ground – no sprinkler system had been installed.[63] In similar protests, other detainees at Woomera and the French camp at Sangatte have sewn their mouths closed. In March 2002 twelve inmates at Woomera symbolically dug their own graves and lay in them as a protest. The poet Abas Amini, a Kurdish refugee in Britain, sewed both his mouth and his eyes closed to protest his ordered deportation to Iran in May 2003. Such resistance nonetheless mimics and reinforces the intent of the camps. Commenting on the protests at Woomera, the Australian minister for immigration, Philip Ruddock, said: "Lip sewing is a practice unknown in our culture. It's something that offends the sensitivities of Australians." That is to say, the very protest by the detained refugees was proof of their barbarism and unfitness for Australian citizenship. The guards at the camp expressed the connections being implied perfectly when they called the protestors "terrorist motherfuckers."[64] The inmates from around Asia are now all terrorists and they are characterized as sexual deviants outside the boundaries of "civilized" behavior as both practioners of political violence and "primitive" protests like lip sewing.

The goal of the camps, then, is to render their inhabitants into the undead, people with no social existence. While the panopticon wanted its prisoners visible at all times, the camps want their inmates to be permanently invisible. The Bush administration has invented a new category of criminal, the "enemy combatant," who can be detained at will because their presumed actions render them without value. In her dissent to the July 9, 2003 ruling by the Fourth Circuit Court of Appeals that upheld the practice (under appeal to the Supreme Court at time of writing), Judge Diana Gribbon Motz argued that the decision allowed "the indefinite detention, without access to a lawyer or the courts, of any American citizen, even one captured on American soil, who the Executive designates an 'enemy combatant.'"[65] The case concerned Yaser Esam Hamdi, an American citizen captured in Afghanistan in 2001. Subsequently, he was held in a military brig and not charged or allowed any access to lawyers, let alone others in the outside world on the basis of a two-page statement by an official in the Defense Department, until a sudden reversal in December 2003. Such procedures recall the early modern practice of the *lettre de cachet* in which the absolute monarch of France was able to order the secret detention of any person he regarded as a threat. Two centuries after the storming of the Bastille, the practice was revived in France at the refugee camp at Sangatte, where people attempting to claim asylum in Europe were detained in primitive conditions. Reporter Djaffer Ait Aoudia quoted an anonymous displaced person in the camp as saying: "We are already dead. Sangatte is the cemetery of the living."[66] Bentham's fear that the ineffective panopticon would turn its inhabitants into ghosts is now government policy. Sangatte itself is now a ghost, as the British and French governments closed it in December 2002 in favor of detaining their refugees at a further remove. The new European strategy to limit refugees and asylum seekers has been borrowed from Australia's Pacific solution. Following British instigation, the European Union is now building a similar remote camp in Croatia, at the village of Trstenik, 30 miles from Zagreb near the town of Dugo Selo. It will hold up to 800 people. The £1 million center will take refugees arriving at British ports and airports from the Balkans and Eastern Europe. No doubt the hope is that this undesirable location will persuade the refugees to accept meager deals to be shipped home or to other, as yet undetermined, countries who might be willing to take them.

As one might expect given the context of re-masculinizing the nation state, the empire of camps is intensely gendered. The camps figure the migrant as male, fecklessly abandoning a family somewhere in the global ghetto, adopting an apparently feminist rhetoric with impressive cynicism. The British Labour immigration minister (since re-shuffled) Lord Rooker declared in May 2002 that: "Most asylum seekers are single men who have deserted their families for economic gain." These remarks were then quoted with approval by the anti-immigration tabloid the *Daily Express* as a validation of its xenophobic campaign. Taken at face value there is an obvious problem with the idea of single men being blamed for abandoning their families, unless the Labour Party has suddenly adopted a Chinese respect for its elders. By leaving their country of origin, non-Western men become single, unlike, for example, Western soldiers or colonial civil servants. As such, their identity becomes suspect and they are in a certain sense instantly convicted of being deviant by the Western nation state. Orientalism has long attributed extravagant and queer sexuality to the East. In Richard Burton's lengthy appendix to his 1885 translation of *The Arabian Nights*, the widest possible geographical definition of the Orient, ranging from Southern Europe via the Middle East and North Africa to the South Seas, was held to be homeland of what he called "Sotadism," or sodomy. This deviant zone ran right through what Burton called Mesopotamia, site of modern Iraq, as it includes the sites of ancient Sodom and Gomorrah. This psycho-geography – the association of geographical space with particular psychic affects – resonates in our own time because digital culture has operated according to what Wendy Hui Kyong Chun has called a "hi-tech Orientalism" of its own, from William Gibson's 1984 novel *Neuromancer*, via the Asianized Los Angeles of *Blade Runner* (the director's cut, 1991) to the Asian affect of the *Matrix* film series.[67] Such apparently random acts as the murder of a British police officer pursuing a supposed terrorist suspect by a young Algerian man in January 2003, are given meaning by this psycho-geographical determinism. In this view, much circulated by British tabloid media, young Islamic men pursue economic or terrorist ambitions with local cost to their abandoned families and global consequences such as September 11. Keeping these men in place sustains both the global economy by maintaining a low-wage female workforce within the "family" structure that Western theorists deem indispensable and prevents the spread of terrorists, newly defined as any Islamic migrant.

Panopticon Inc.

The camps are themselves the center of an expanding transnational industry. The first level of opportunity is the privatization of detention and other corrections worldwide. Even greater is the opportunity presented by the denationalization of the nation state in Iraq to rebuild what the American army and air force destroyed, while enabling the modernization of the oil fields, a market that has been cornered by the multinational Halliburton. Had the so-called road map succeeded, there would have been another such market in Palestine. As this mode of capitalizing destruction is still in its infancy, let's here consider the private prison empire. The British camp at Yarl's Wood was initially run by the private security firm Group 4, while all five Australian camps for detainees were managed by Australasian Correctional Management, a subsidiary of the US penal giant Wackenhut Corrections. Wackenhut, now renamed the GEO Group, manages 61 correctional and detentional centers in North America, Europe, Puerto Rico, Australia, South Africa and New Zealand, generating annual revenues in excess of $500 million and a 14.1 percent profit increase in 2001. According to its own website, Wackenhut deals in "prisoner transportation, electronic monitoring for home detainees, correctional health care and mental health services." Like any other multinational, Wackenhut sends its capital where profits are to be made and is subject to the monopolizing character of globalization, leading it in 2002 to close an "unprofitable" prison in Arkansas in favor of a 3024-bed facility in South Africa. So successful were these strategies that Wackenhut was itself taken over by the $2.5 billion Danish corporation Group 4 Falck,[68] resulting in a dramatic 97 percent increase in net income in the first quarter of 2002 for Wackenhut as a separate division within Group 4. More generally, this concentration of private corrections has engendered the unnoticed creation of a global empire of incarceration in the hands of corporations, not governments.[69] Wackenhut claims 24 percent of the global market for private corrections (www.wcc-corrections.com), while its rival, the Corrections Corporation of

America (www.correctionscorp.com), claims to operate more corrections facilities in the US than all but four states and the federal government. This carceral regime has its own communications network, relying on websites like www.corrections.com and www.prisonstoday.com to keep it posted of new technology, to swap ideas on bulletin boards and catch up with the news.

A crisis in American prisons seems possible, as the withdrawal of private prisons has coincided with the execution of punitive sentencing laws, generating a vast explosion in prison inmate numbers. With prisons already full, some non-violent offenders are being freed, sent into drug treatment programs, or not imprisoned in the first place because there is nowhere to put them. Even in jail-happy California, non-violent offenders in Los Angeles were released early in 2003 as the county, facing a $170 million budget deficit, was caught between its desire to incarcerate drug users and illegal immigrants, as well as three-time offenders, and the limits of state budgets in the current recession. Nonetheless Wackenhut posted an optimistic forecast of continued expansion to its website in 2003, due to the war on terrorism and the continued determination of the federal government to maintain detention as its primary strategy. Indeed, in 2003 the US federal system became the largest single incarcerator, holding over 172,000 inmates compared to roughly 160,000 in both California and Texas. As the states seek to reduce their prison populations, Attorney General John Ashcroft instructed federal prosecutors in September 2003 to set aside plea bargains and aim for the sternest possible penalties. Wackenhut and other private prison corporations win either way. Its share price rose by more than 50 percent in the first six months of 2003, allowing it to repurchase all shares from Group 4 Falck by August 2003.[70] At the same time, Wackenhut sold its British operations at a profit to its former partner Serco and renamed itself the GEO Group, with headquarters in Boca Raton, Florida. The *South Florida Business Journal*, which covers the area, represents GEO's profit as the result of "opening its Lawrenceville Correctional Facility in Virginia in March, a strengthened Australian dollar, [and] improved occupancy rates."

The GEO Group/Wackenhut's share price (GEO continues to use the old Wackenhut designator WHC on the New York Stock Exchange) has more than doubled since these maneuvers, which gives some indication of how powerful market flexibility is for the new global corporations. It is difficult, as the Enron situation has shown, to fully understand what is in fact happening in these flows of capital. How Wackenhut repurchased itself is hard to comprehend in common-sense terms. Meanwhile, due to a cut in budget, Texas and six other state prison systems are offering their inmates a reduced calorie diet with only two meals a day on holidays and weekends, making it clear who the losers are in this game.

Camp Iraq

From the point of view of its own citizens, Iraq is now functioning as a camp. Large portions of the country are under constant curfew, and thousands are being detained, often in Saddam's old prisons. Media reports in early 2004 suggested that some 13,000 people were being held without charge or the possibility of trial in Iraq. Within Camp Iraq is the camp of camps, the so-called "Sunni triangle," the middle third of the country that contains the capital Baghdad. The camp effect can be observed at several levels. In everyday life, the sense of loss in the popular mood, the devastation of public services, and the restrictions on personal movement deprive Iraqis of citizenship in their own country. While these conditions may be seen as temporary, the occupation is an extraordinary effort to convert a nation state previously functioning as a command economy into a denationalized zone for global capital. Whether as a state of transition or permanent condition, the country has become a supervised and hostile refugee camp on the model of Israel's permanent war with the Palestinians in the Gaza Strip and on the West Bank.

At the time of writing, Iraqi everyday life has become notably worse since the war and occupation began. Supplies of water and electricity remain extremely uncertain, while even gasoline is very hard to come by in this oil-rich nation due both to deliberate sabotage and the delapidated equipment of the Iraqi oil-fields. Although the war was declared over by George W. Bush in May 2003, there was no effort to restore regular telecommunications until US intelligence determined that the insurgents were not communicating by phone. At the same time, this policy had the effect of cutting off ordinary Iraqis from the outside world. The consequences were noticeable. When US forces were attacked in Samara in November 2003, they claimed to have killed 54 *fedayeen*, or militiamen. Locals claimed, by contrast, that only seven or eight bystanders had been killed. Robert Fisk of the London *Independent* verified that only nine bodies were in the mortuary but the US military claimed that fighters' bodies would not be sent to such an official facility. Of course, one cannot distinguish the truth of these accounts at a distance but the simple existence of conflicting accounts adds a degree of complexity that US officials would prefer to suppress. Nonetheless bystanders are killed almost daily in shoot-outs between the US army and the Iraqi opposition forces, as well as by car bombs and suicide bombers. One Iraqi anonymously quoted in the *New York Times* placed his people firmly in the empire of camps: "Saddam Hussein killed all the Iraqis. Even the ones who are alive are now dead."[71] This despair is extending to the occupying troops, with three suicides by US soldiers being reported as of November 2003 and some 500 requiring mental health treatment.[72] In the Bush administration's 2003 request for $87 billion to refinance Iraq, it was noticeable that $500 million was budgeted for the construction of several new high security prisons, as opposed to only $100 million for new housing in a country devastated by two decades of war. Both provisions were later removed by Congress as a symbolic gesture of oversight, reducing the cost by a nominal $1.7 billion, while the loss of new housing further depleted the benefits of this package for ordinary Iraqis.

Restrictions on personal movement are now similar to those in the West Bank. Traffic barriers and curfews have become a part of Iraqi everyday life since the beginning of the occupation in May 2003, just as they are in Palestine. Increased traffic control in Baghdad has led to school runs of a few kilometers taking hours, in a fashion all too familiar to Palestinians who have to use a separate road network to Israelis. In December 2003, the US army instigated a new high-profile assault on the insurgency that culminated with the arrest of Saddam Hussein. News reports described the way in which Iraqi towns and villages were turned into de facto camps. For example, the 7000 inhabitants of Abu Hishma were subjected to a fifteen-hour curfew, a razor-wire fence, and identity cards with text in English only, after an attack on American forces was determined to have come from their town. The razor fence allows only one way in and out of the town and carries the extraordinary sign: "The fence is here for your protection. Do not approach or try to cross, or you will be shot." One local man said to a *New York Times* reporter: "I see no difference between us and the Palestinians."[73] Veteran intelligence reporter Seymour Hersh suggested that the US is taking advice from the Israelis on counter-insurgency policy and that some Israelis may be secretly deployed as advisers.[74] In this view, it is no coincidence that concurrent with the occupation of Iraq has been the construction of a high barrier by Israel along an arbitrary line of security that exceeds its 1967 borders.[75] Towns such as Qalqilya are surrounded on three sides, creating a Palestinian ghetto. As has happened consistently since the United States became "Israelized" in its adoption of exclusionary security state policies, Israel has refused American entreaties to desist from this practice. As there is a similar barrier along the US border with Mexico at San Diego that stretches for miles at a height of sixteen feet, it could also be said that the Americans initiated the policy.

While these strategies are held to be short-term responses to the insurgency, the longer-term strategy for Iraq – insofar as there is one – is for it to become a denationalized zone for the operation of global capital. Saskia Sassen has argued that globalization entails a "de-nationalizing" of time and space.[76] In Sassen's view, this denationalization has hitherto taken place for the most part in certain privileged global cities as a series of exemptions that "makes possible the hypermobility of financial capital on the global scale."

The detain-and-deport system of the empire of camps reinforces this mobility of capital in two decisive ways. First, it restricts the workforce to those locales desired by capital. To meet this demand, a migrant workforce of no fewer than 100 million people has been created in China.[77] Working for between $50 and $120 a month, this fluid industrial reserve army of globalization produces the low-cost goods the new economy needs. Now with the invasion of Iraq we have seen the denationalization of the nation state, in part to ensure the free flow of primary extractive resources, in this case oil. Even if some of the political actors did not believe this to be their motive, the effect of the war has been to collapse the possibility of Iraq acting as a legal personality, while restoring the oil reserves of the country to the international market. Second, it restores the privilege of the one-third world over the two-thirds world, such that the perquisites of the Western nation state have been reinforced to a remarkable extent by the denationalization of the two-thirds world's nation states. Finally, the wholesale privatization of Iraqi government assets, widely considered to be in breach of the conventions of occupation, has transformed the Iraqi economy from state-controlled centralism to the current orthodoxy of deregulated market capitalism almost overnight. Even the occupation has been privatized with over 10,000 private military contractors operating in Iraq at the end of 2003. For example, the British firm Global Risk Strategies has more than 1000 personnel in Iraq, including Gurkas, Fijian militiamen and, allegedly, ex-SAS men.[78] The relics of the old British Empire are now being used to support the new regime of empire. However, this is not just an ideological project but one with substantial financial rewards. The US Army estimates that at least $30 billion of the $87 billion appropriated by the Bush administration to sustain the occupation of Iraq will go to private corporations. In this sense, the Iraq war was fought as a key part of the consolidation of reactionary globalization, rather than for the now-discredited rationale of eliminating weapons of mass destruction.

Closing global circuits

Closed circuit television (CCTV) has become the dominant visual technology of the empire of camps. The standard CCTV system connects a series of analog cameras to a bank of monitors using fiber-optic cables. These systems are now some 30 years old and, on their introduction, were quickly critiqued by artists like Peter Campus, Dan Graham and Bruce Nauman. Today CCTV is an entire industry with a variety of products from the low-end video camera recording to a VCR in a store to on-line digital systems. There are estimated to be at least 25 million CCTV cameras in operation today, almost all in the advanced capitalist societies, with some 10 percent of the total in Britain alone. The Situationist website notbored.org has mapped a number of North American cities by means of their CCTV cameras and offers tours of surveillance facilities in Manhattan. As technology, the CCTV system allows a single viewer – or a computer in many cases – to survey a variety of remote locations that far exceeds the capacity of biological vision. The images are not available to anyone else, although they can be taped for evidentiary purposes. Many American trials now feature such tapes. At the everyday level, CCTV monitors traffic speeds, issues tickets for speeding and has successfully been deployed to regulate London traffic. At this level, there can be certain benefits from the technology, such as monitoring for drug dealers in local neighborhoods, or effective enforcement of traffic quietening schemes. Like any system of power, CCTV enables as well as represses. Symbolically, however, its ascendancy represents the end of the nascent network society that was based above all else on free-flow, whether of capital, images information or people and the return to a closed system like that of the Cold War.

In July 2002, Samsung introduced its new "high-impact armored dome line" of CCTVs, guaranteed indestructible and recommended as "ideal for use in environments such as prisons or educational campuses." Samsung was not doing this to make a witty reference to Foucault. Schools across the United States have installed such systems at an average cost of $30,000 a school. In Biloxi, Mississippi, the school district was persuaded to spend an astonishing $1.2 million to install digital cameras in each of 500 classrooms, in a state that regularly ranks last in assessments of educational attainment. In order to pay for it, the state issued bonds, tapped gambling revenue and appropriated federal funds intended to connect schools to the Internet.[79] This intersection of prisons with schools shows that the CCTV is the realization of Bentham's once impossible dream of a single visual system for a variety of disciplinary institutions. No doubt most factories, prisons, military barracks and schools (Foucault's classic examples of disciplinary institutions) are now being surveyed by CCTV cameras. Many such institutions are turning to on-line and digital systems using a special chip called a charge-coupled device to record the images produced by the cameras. Two PC servers can now do the same recording work as 100 VCRs, a good measure of the transformation of the visual economy by digitization. The information can be transmitted around an already existing local area network, saving more outlay. Consequently they are popular both with organizations like schools and shopping malls looking to provide security at the lowest cost and with police. When the US goes to a heightened level of terrorist alert, digital CCTV networks of this kind are activated in the Washington DC subway system, at intersections and major tourist sites. Unlike analog systems, which usually record from only a small number of cameras at any one time, the digital systems record from all their cameras all the time. The low cost of disk space means that security records can be kept for longer, allowing for detection and investigation long after the event.

For all the similarities to Bentham's earlier idea, the culture of CCTV is radically different from nineteenth-century Utilitarianism with its aim of the greatest good for the greatest number. The goal now is the least bad from the fewest offenders. The technological accomplishment represented by CCTV should not so dazzle us that we overlook the dramatic cultural shift it entails. Like the panopticon, CCTV is based on all-seeing technology, but the difference between the two is that while CCTV really does see (almost) every-thing, it prevents nothing. It has no goals other than to detect. One of the most striking examples of this paradox was seen on September 11, when Mohammed Atta, a known FBI suspect, was filmed by CCTV getting onto a plane in Boston, which he then hijacked and flew into the World Trade Center. This airport footage is now familiar to millions but did nothing to stop the events themselves. It is possible to argue that a correlation between known suspects and visual surveillance is just a matter of time. But the technological barriers that would need to be overcome to make this possible are very significant – to take just two, cameras would have to be capable of instant face recognition, and correlation with databases would need constant updating. However, Jay Walker, the founder of Priceline.com, has sought to make the entire Internet into a surveillance tool as a means of overcoming these objections. In his proposed US Homeguard system, a network of

Figure 3.1 Armored CCTV camera
(Courtesy of Extreme CCTV)

web cams would be trained on the perimeters of all potential installations that might be the target of terrorist attack in the US (www.ushomeguard.com). A floating army of web users, composed of students and military families, would be used to check the images for the presence of intruders. Paid only minimum wage, these guardians would themselves be subject to surveillance as the system would test them by sending fake pictures of intruders every ten to fifteen shots. The system claims that a detection and verification would thus take place in 30 seconds, placing an astonishing trust in the data network. The implications for civil liberties of US Homeguard and other such schemes are still more worrying. So we need to ask what kind of work that technology is doing now.

This cultural work is being undertaken throughout the visual arts and media. The viewpoint of CCTV was aestheticized by Mike Figgis' film *Timecode* (2000) that presented its real-time four-way split-screen as its prime attraction. The film was as much a formal

Figure 3.2 Educational CCTV
(Courtesy of Extreme CCTV)

test of the viewer's ability to operate as a CCTV security guard –
look! there's something interesting – as it was a standard narrative. Nonetheless, it seemed that an effort had been made, despite
the dotcom style "real-time" shooting, to ensure that only one of
the four images was presenting something of importance at any
given moment. The inevitable sex scene alluded to the extensive
use on the Internet of spy-cams and other digital cameras to
provide paying users with voyeuristic sights, ranging from changing
rooms to bathrooms and outright sex scenes. This unappealing
undercurrent to netlife stands in relation to *Timecode* as the development of VHS video technology by the pornography industry in
the 1970s did to its adoption by artists and others. The performance artist Coco Fusco, who has called attention to these uses of
CCTV, used the format in her piece *Dolores*, which restaged the
interrogation of a union activist in a Mexican *maquilladora* factory.
Unlike *Timecode* with its four locked-in images, *Dolores* mimics the
earlier CCTV systems in cycling from one camera to the next.
The result is that just as Dolores is being interrogated, our view
switches to a deserted corridor. Unlike Figgis and the pay-per-
view sites, Fusco refuses to put her spectator in the position of
all-seeing power. Ironically, the panoptic technology she uses
refuses to allow the viewer the position of the panoptic jailer, able
to see all the prisoners all the time. As surveillance has gone extensively digital, the hactivist Radical Software Group has made
available a version of the FBI digital surveillance software called
Carnivore. Both programs scan data such as email, user-groups
and listservs for specific terms or areas. The RSG version,
CarnivorePE, can be used to create artistic and acoustic events.
Its piece *Police State* reverses the power dynamics by converting a
given data packet on US domestic terrorism to a short-wave radio
signal that controls the model police cars.

As the RSG put it: "Thus the police become puppets of their
own surveillance." Before long the cars are crashing into each other
and disrupting their own attempt to represent order. The entertainment and surveillance uses of CCTV came together in
television coverage of the Iraq war. All the US news channels made

extensive use of fixed-camera views of Baghdad, nearly always showing very little of interest. MSNBC, for example, showed a view of what seemed to be a parking garage. The "liveness" of the image was here of interest solely because it might at any given moment start relaying a deadly bombing or missile attack. When the raids began, CNN would often switch to a four-way locked-in divided screen, showing four different views of the city in the hope that its viewers would miss as few impacts as possible. Its competitors at Fox News and MSNBC quickly imitated the format, although the network news stayed mostly with the traditional single-image format. Watching such four-way images was neither news nor entertainment but a form of work. In effect it was job training for remote surveillance like that proposed by US Homeguard. For all that, the only striking moment I observed in hours of such surveillance came from a sound, the sound of a large quantity of breaking glass after a bomb had dropped somewhere off-screen.

The war unfolded against the spread of the global craze for reality television, in which people voluntarily subject themselves to surveillance for the entertainment of others. Reality television is, of course, anything but real. It is carefully staged in selected locations with screened participants, using the viewpoint of CCTV as its dramatic signature. Its reality stems from its displaced acknowledgement of the closed-circuit culture that has come into being. A now-established formula presents the audience with the "actual" thoughts of the competitors, who are subjected to a relentless surveillance not to make them better people but to catch them doing something wrong, or, preferably, sexual. These shows, like *Big Brother* and *Survivor*, are nonetheless a counterpoint to the disinterested surveillance of the empire. For here being watched makes a difference: at the end of each week's episodes, one person is voted off and at last a winner emerges. In this scenario, everyday life is a spectacle that cannot be ignored. At the same time, the hermetic environment in which the competition unfolds acknowledges the return of the closed world, just as *Who Wants to Be a Millionaire?* spoke to the unfettered capitalist ambition of the

Figure 3.3 Jonah Brucker-Cohen, *PoliceState*, 2003
(Courtesy of Jonah Brucker-Cohen, http://www.coin-operated.com)

Internet boom. The degree to which the events are manipulated by the producers in the name of "reality" shows that what Roland Barthes once called the "reality effect" no longer pertains in the apparently realistic medium of television. Just as it is taken for granted that a *Big Brother* competitor misrepresents his or her motives to fellow participants, so viewers take it as read that the visual reality offered on television is a carefully staged manipulation. Yet it is still real in the sense that contemporary reality is dominated by surveillance and a sense of closed boundaries, a new reality that creates new desires.

Global gender trouble

Like on-line spy cameras, *Big Brother* globally has come to rely on the sexual interactions of its participants to sustain interest. Swedish and German versions of the series became notorious for the frequency of such events, but in the United States the first sexual encounter on *Big Brother* was shown in July 2003, fittingly enough only to subscribers of the 24/7 on-line service. In order to enhance the thrill of delayed and enacted sexual desire, reality TV has now moved extensively into dating shows. As the thrill waned, 2003 versions seemed to incorporate a cultural studies critique into the show. *Love or Money* offered cash incentives to participants, as well as the presumed love interest, as if acknowledging that marriage is often as much a commercial as emotional institution. With the launch of *Boy Meets Boy*, the implication that heterosexuality is so diminished that it needs the assistance of a television show to arrange partners was addressed by taking on the gay male market. At the same time, the show is heavily laced with homophobia as some of the participants are straight and viewers are encouraged to separate them from the "real" queers. Here, as elsewhere on gay-themed American television like the sit-com *Will and Grace* or the reality show *Queer Eye for the Straight Guy*, gay is taken to mean a white man, either with muscles or a waspish wit, rendering lesbians, transgender people and other alternative modes of sexuality invisible. Nonetheless, it is striking how pursuing the theme of discipline and surveillance in contemporary culture seems to at a certain point inevitably to intersect with discussions about sexuality and gender identity.

It is clear that this gender trouble is puzzling to the ruling elites of the empire. On the one hand, the "West" wants to represent itself as progressive as compared to the barbaric "East," represented by the veiling of women and sexual discrimination of all kinds. To this end, the notorious 1986 Supreme Court ruling in *Bowers* v. *Hardwick* upholding the criminalization of sodomy in Texas was revisited and overturned in *Lawrence et al.* v. *Texas* (2003). In his majority opinion, Justice Kennedy began by emphasizing the pre-eminence of freedom: "Liberty protects the person from unwarranted government intrusion into a dwelling place or other private places." Kennedy thus offered a theory of Western liberty that depends on the notion of privacy, rather than an overweening state morality. The right to privacy is in fact a conservative viewpoint that Kennedy used instrumentally to defend queer sexuality by explicitly making use of the pro-choice privacy ruling in *Roe* v. *Wade* (1973). In this view, the fourteenth amendment offers a right to privacy that was deployed in terms of reproductive choice and should be now extended to sexual relationships. In what seems an all but hysterical dissent, but is in fact a staple of radical right rhetoric, Justice Antonin Scalia envisaged the end of the standard family, when he claimed that the decision would invalidate "criminal laws against fornication, bigamy, adultery, adult incest, bestiality, and obscenity." An editorial in the *New York Times* pointed out that Scalia's arguments were deployed in 1967 when Virginia repealed its law banning cross-ethnic marriages.[80] Indeed, when the Massachussetts Supreme Court decided in 2003 that there were no constitutional grounds to prohibit same-sex marriage, their decision relied strongly on precedent of inter-racial marriage. The White House has taken a strong position against same-sex civil unions and marriages, playing the racialized and gendered codes for what it hopes to be maximum political advantage. Now that same-sex unions have been recognized in France, Britain and Canada, the Bush administration finds itself in what, for a Protestant fundamentalist group, can only be an unholy alliance with the Vatican against them.

These attempts to restrain the flows and desires of contemporary culture are themselves challenged by the expression of the digital right to privacy, defined by media theorist Roger Clarke as being "the freedom from unreasonable constraints on the construction of one's identity."[81] As befits a network society, connections continue to exist between the means of surveillance, the place of the individual within the nation state and questions of difference that are not susceptible to erasure by Executive Order of the White House. Indeed, the Internet itself seems to be in the process of redefinition. Openness is increasingly figured as a mode of democratic expression, rather than being restricted to the availability of free software. Pioneered by sites like nettime.org and open-democracy.net, this new net activism offers a means to redefine "free" as freedom of information, expression and intellectual exchange. Most strikingly, the Internet has become a medium of communication to enable real-world activities, ranging from the Dada-esque Flash Mobs of 2003 to the political activism of Howard Dean's campaign for the 2004 Democratic Presidential nomination and the formation of social and activist groups of all kinds via sites like meetup.com. Meetup uses the web as a means for like-minded people to meet up with each other, not in the now familiar territory of chatrooms and bulletin boards, but face to face. On-line virtual reality now seems less attractive and less potentially open than actual social space. The Internet is becoming a means to facilitate what Ricardo Dominguez of Electronic Disturbance Theatre calls "encounter" and "dialogue," terms he has appropriated from the Zapatista resistance movement in Chiapas, Mexico, who used the web to make their cause discussed globally.[82]

For global capital to succeed in consolidating itself in these most reactionary of forms, it will have to continue its assault on the network society, a perhaps impossible project. Consequently, the Pentagon's much-derided Total Information Awareness project (subsequently renamed Terrorist Information Awareness) is central to the effort. This office is a part of the Defense Advanced Research Project Agency, or DARPA, whose main achievement was the ARPA-net, created in the 1970s as a means of maintaining military communications even in the event of a nuclear war, now seen to be the backbone of the contemporary Internet. DARPA is now trying to put the genie that ARPA released back into the bottle. At the same time, the Internet proved its value as a political organizing tool and meeting place in its own right during the opposition to the Gulf War. During the war, websites and web logs were a crucial source of alternative information. Internet fundraising now offers a way for alternative candidates like Howard Dean to make an impact in the presidential election, albeit in that case with a very dotcom outcome. What this suggests is that, on and off line, there is a choice between passive consumption, accepting security as the primary goal; or an active citizenship that argues for the right to privacy as being central to digital activism, women's reproductive rights and the right to queer sexuality. While radicals have spent much time lamenting the decline of the public sphere, it increasingly appears that upholding an anti-sexist, anti-homophobic, pro-activist, pro-copyleft private sphere is the vital terrain for the present.

Ethics in the open city

Such rhetorical flourishes are easy enough to make. The undead of the empire of camps remain in an unacknowledged limbo, forced to learn the techniques of the specter, to replace ontology with hauntology. Such hauntology has its own spectral history and there are lessons to be learnt from the ghosts that have gone before us. In her essay introducing Walter Benjamin's essays, Hannah Arendt quoted Franz Kafka at the opening of a section entitled "Dark Times." Kafka wrote in his diary for October 19, 1921:

> Anyone who cannot cope with life while he is alive needs one hand to ward off a little his despair over his fate . . . but with his other hand he can jot down what he sees among the ruins, for he sees different and more things than the others; after all, he is dead in his own lifetime and the real survivor.[83]

This undead survivor sees not with an all-powerful gaze nor as the object of a totalizing panopticism but as a person trying to negotiate what Achille Mbembe has called "an ensemble of ways of living, representing and experiencing contemporaneousness, while at the same time, inscribing this experience in the mentality, language and experience of historical time."[84] That is to say that the contemporary is a privileged and guarded space to which not everyone has access. The empire of camps is designed to exclude the global majority from the contemporary, as capital defines the contemporary.

In order to find out how those of us interested in an open, networked, or connected model of society might begin to think it through, there is a need for a refuge from their contemporary. Such refuge is transitory and interstitial, as imagined in Roberto

Rossellini's classic film *Citta aperta* (Open City) made in 1945.
Partly shot in secret while the Nazis still occupied Rome, the city
of the title, the film does not represent its openness, meaning a
demilitarized city. By the end of the film, the Nazis have in fact
broken a Resistance group in the city and executed their leaders.
The open city, demilitarized and therefore potentially a place of
refuge, was, in the film and elsewhere, yet to come. It offers the
counterpoint to the closed system of contemporary global capitalism, just as Paul Edwards argued that the "green world" was the
counter to the closed world of the Cold War.[85] It arises from a
sense of ethical obligation that is as ancient as religion and as
contemporary as the present crisis. For Edward Said, hospitality
is central to scholarship, such that "the interpreter's mind actively
makes a place in it for a foreign 'other.'"[86] His evocation of the
moment of openness was anticipated by the philosopher Emmanuel
Levinas in his meditation on what he calls the "poetry of Derrida,"
meaning the philosophy of deconstruction. Levinas created what I
think of as a prose poem, set in the crisis of France in 1940 as the
retreating French army passes through an apparently normal town

> where, an hour later, everything is deconstructed and devas-
> tated: . . . In these in-between days, a symbolic episode:
> somewhere in between Paris and Alençon, a half-drunk barber
> used to invite soldiers who were passing on the road to come
> and have a free shave in his shop; the "lads" he used to call
> them. . . . With his two companions, he shaved them free of
> charge – and it was today. The essential procrastination – the
> future *différance* – was reabsorbed into the present. Time
> came to its end with the end of the interim period of France.[87]

In this space, the present is finally present to itself. The space
between the retreating French army and the arriving Germans
paradoxically created an open city of refuge. The open city is a
moment in which identity is not subject to deferral, a space in
which exchange is not mediated by the cash nexus and time itself
becomes open. It is enacted performatively, in everyday life, in

relation to the body. Levinas's image recalls other such moments in war. On Christmas Day 1914, a British barber set up in no man's land and offered shaves to both sides in the truce called by the enlisted men over the heads of their commanding officers.[88] The barbers of Kabul offered men free shaves in 2001 during the interim between the departure of the Taliban and the arrival of the US-sponsored forces. This shave was of course a political riposte to the enforcement of beards by the Taliban and one man, who took a shave, said that he would grow it back but "this one is for me" rather than the Taliban. This refashioning of self-image was what Rancière would call the emergence of the possibility of a (visual) subject in the brief absence of the police. What matters is not so much the masculine trope of the barber, as the symbolic openness, the hospitality, the space of freedom. This renewed convergence on the ethical questions of hospitality and refuge could not be more urgently contemporary, yet, as I think Said and Derrida would agree, it also returns the intellectual endeavor to its ancient beginnings.

The open city has to begin by insisting on the ancient rights of refuge, asylum and sanctuary. Levinas revisited the theme of the open city in a chapter of his study of the Talmud devoted to the concept of the "city of refuge."[89] According to the sages of the Babylonian Talmud – that is to say, the Talmud as written by the Babylonian rabbis during the long Jewish residence in Babylon after the formal Jewish captivity of the sixth century, a place of writing that resonates here – certain verses of the Torah mandate that those who kill without intending to do so, objectively guilty of killing but subjectively innocent of a crime, should have places of refuge constructed for them to protect them from vengeance. These places must be populous, well watered and located in market districts, away from traffic in arms. They sound a little like an idealized version of the modern suburbs with which we began. "Life," concludes Levinas, "can thus only mean life worthy of the name" (page 42). There can be no equivocation that the Law itself provides a sufficient refuge. Derrida has revisited these pages in his recent essay "On Cosmopolitanism" (1997) in support of the specific project of the city of refuge, and also as a key component of imaging a new Europe as part of a cosmopolitanism that can draw on a wide range of traditions and texts. This cosmopolitanism is a reworking of Kant's theory of the cosmopolitical in the era in which "the police become omnipresent and spectral."[90] The actually existing European Union seems rather far from this cosmopolitanism, as do the United States. The point here is not to suggest that the France of 1940 or the Afghanistan of 2001 were cities of refuge or otherwise desirable locations, whether permanently or for a moment. It is to explore the sense that the present can only be present and the subject actively contemporary in the anarchic absence of the police. Without claiming to reform what we cannot affect, we should try to see that our classes, our centers for the humanities, perhaps at times even our universities, become such places of refuge from the empire of camps.

Afterword: Afterimages

So, in April 2004, a year after the statue of Saddam was pulled down live on international television, what do things look like? These remarks are a snapshot within a process that is still in motion. The US is set on its course of pulling out by June 30, 2004, in name at least, well in advance of the November elections. What they are leaving behind seems increasingly to be a volatile and dangerous situation that is unlikely to generate the "Washington on the Euphrates" fantasy of right-wing think tanks that was the model for the invasion. This month the death toll of American military passed 700 for the entire conflict, causing public confidence in the war in the US to drop to 35 percent, the same level as during the 1968 Tet offensive in the Vietnam war. While 126 US soldiers were reported killed this month, over 1300 Iraqis have died, with some reports estimating 350 women and children killed in Fallujah alone. The index that US control is slipping comes in the form of images that are no longer so tightly controlled that they seem to have no meaning. In fact, compelling images are crossing our screens daily this month from the violent attack on four Blackwater USA security guards in Fallujah, to the frequent images of scared hostages, and the alternance of cheering crowds around burning Coalition vehicles and weeping ones around coffins. An intrepid website has even obtained the jealously concealed photographs of dead US service personnel returning to Dover Air Base (http://www.thememoryhole.org). Perhaps the most astonishing sight was that of Shia and Sunni Muslims worshipping together in Baghdad, united against the occupation, a sight only slightly less unlikely than seeing the Reverend Ian Paisley (a radical Ulster Protestant) taking Catholic mass. The month ended with the photographs of torture by British and American troops that seemed to return Iraq to its point of departure before the invasion. What the military-visual planners forgot was that all Western weapons deployed in the field are subject to "blowback," being used against their originators.

On April 10, 2004, the anniversary of the statue toppling, photographs of Moqtada al-Sadr, the radical Shi'ite cleric, were attached to the new statue representing liberty that has been erected in place of Saddam's monument. Marines, who a year ago demolished that monument, were seen removing the photos. Meanwhile a Humvee circled behind them, broadcasting threats to shoot any armed person on sight. Al-Sadr commands a militia known as the Mahdi army. One fighter was photographed wearing a reversed balaclava with a green and white Arabic inscription on his forehead. Despite his strategy, you could still read the Nike logo on the inside of the black balaclava and, equally clearly, you could see that it was a fake. In that photograph is an entire history of globalization. The global brands, like Nike, were the engineers of global production and distribution, attracting both intense desire for their products and equally sharp resentment of the wealth they produced and the unfair labor practices they embodied. This fighter embodied the contradiction by both owning a "Nike," albeit a fake, and repurposing it to serve as part of his uniform in an anti-American militia. Yet for his American audience his anonymity is a reinforcement of long-standing Orientalist tropes of the fearsome Islamic warrior that date back to the medieval wars in Spain and Turkey. For a viewer able to read Arabic, the dominant message in the photograph would probably be the slogan wrapped around his forehead that was left untranslated in the Western sources I saw.

By now the story of the war is both somewhat clearer and yet to be fully told. On the one hand, it is clear that Iraq did not in fact continue to hold so-called weapons of mass destruction, the purported cause of the invasion. Equally, it is clear that the decision to invade Iraq was taken by November 2001, even as Western leaders continued to assert in March 2003 that the final choice had yet to be made. While the Spanish electorate responded to the obfuscations of the Popular Party, a strong supporter of the war, concerning the Madrid bombings of 2004 by returning a Socialist government, it is not yet clear whether Bush, Blair and Howard will pay a similar electoral price for their earlier deceptions. Spanish troops were immediately set to withdraw from Iraq, prompting Honduras and the Dominican Republic (two of the minor members of the Coalition) to follow suit. The case that it was always worth getting rid of Saddam, even if the reasons given for doing so at the time were false, has been pushed so energetically that no decisive swing has yet been seen in the Anglo-Australian-American electorate. Of the war itself, we still know relatively little. It has been estimated that Western journalists witnessed about 100 air raids, mostly on Baghdad, out of a total of over 20,000.[1] On the specific example of the fighting in al-Hillah discussed in this book, Human Rights Watch has discovered that the cluster bombs were in fact launched by the US 3rd Infantry Division using multiple launch rocket vehicles.[2] Only one salvo was actually fired but that delivered 3864 "bomblets," each with considerable power. Broader information about the numbers of Iraqi casualties remains obscure or unavailable. It took a reporter for National Public Radio months of research to even come up with an approximate number of American wounded because the Pentagon insists that the information has not been collated. The information revolution was not all it was cracked up to be.

In the American suburbs, there are small signs of change. While Wal-Mart continues to dominate the retail sector, it is not doing so unchallenged. In April 2004, voters in Inglewood, California, voted down a ballot initiative that would have given Wal-Mart immunity from all local ordinances, such as environmental and labor regulation, in exchange for opening a vast store in a depressed inner-city area. If the store is true to form, it will now try and open the store as close to Inglewood as possible but Southern California labor is trying very hard to keep Wal-Mart out of at least one metropolitan area. Wal-Mart now has an annual turnover that, were it a gross domestic product, would rank it thirtieth among world nations. Now that its dominance is so clear, Wal-Mart has become the subject of academic interest with a major conference on Wal-Mart as the new Microsoft being held this month at the University of California, Santa Barbara.[3] Hummers continue to sell well, although not quite as well as during the war. On Long Island they are becoming a regular sight, now blending in with the other over-sized SUVs as part of the suburban drive-scape. With national reports indicating that 60 percent of Americans are overweight or obese (and these are generous standards), the fast food industry has had its friends in Congress pass a law indemnifying them against potential lawsuits. At the same time, McDonald's and the other chains are falling over themselves to offer "healthy" salads, although the high-fat dressing and croutons take the edge off the practice. Houses continue to expand, with the latest trend being to "supersize" your house. This involves taking a standard house or cottage and rebuilding it into the largest structure the plot will support. As Long Island was originally laid out as a "garden suburb," most houses are detached in at least one-third of an acre of land, giving contractors plenty of space to build. Local authorities, whose corruption is legendary, fall over themselves to give planning permission for these houses, the increased size of which generates extra property tax revenue for the state and county.

Alongside these changes, the empire of camps continues to flourish. The revived insurrection in Iraq has turned cities like Fallujah and Najaf into camps within the camp, reinforcing the sense of intractable moral deviance that motivates the system. Following the model of the West Bank barrier, US Marines have built a 200-mile-long, fifteen-feet-high barrier on the Iraq–Syria border in order to keep out "foreign" fighters, who were blamed for the unrest before the al-Sadr-inspired uprising. As the US continues to adopt Israeli tactics, such as the use of Apache helicopters to assassinate opposition leaders, it was no surprise to see the Likud leader Ariel Sharon score a triumph by having the American government passively endorse his new segregating scheme. In Sharon's model, Gaza is to become a separate camp, cut off from the Palestinian Authority. With the Hamas leadership assassinated and all major services still controlled by the Israelis, the withdrawal is in name only. Meanwhile the West Bank, significantly diminished by the permanent annexation of major settlements, is hidden behind the Israeli barrier. For the Israeli writer David Grossman, Sharon's government has produced "death as a way of life," the spectral existence produced by the empire of camps. Yet even he cannot envisage the bi-national solution supported by Edward Said and many others in which all the territory under dispute would become one secular nation state with freedom of religion. Grossman could not imagine being a member of a "Jewish minority" in such a state, even though to conceive of this state in terms of permanent ethnic/religious divides would be to miss its entire purpose. It is precisely this fear of an "Arab majority" that Sharon has exploited in his Gaza plan that has already been endorsed by Labor leader Shimon Peres. All Western leaders, including Senator John Kerry, have pre-emptively endorsed the plan before the Israeli Knesset has even debated it. The only group who may oppose it, ironically, is Sharon's own Likud party, for whom any concession of land is sacrilege.

Reflecting this strength, global corrections corporations continue to flourish. The GEO Group (formerly Wackenhut Corrections) had revenues of $617.5 million in 2003, a 9 percent increase over 2002, generating a net profit of $43.5 million. These figures are surrounded, as ever, by a fog of write-offs, deductions and so on. Australians who thought that Wackenhut had been deprived of their contract to run detention centers for refugees in 2002 soon discovered that Group 4 Falck had simply switched the operation to another part of its conglomerate. In early 2004, the Geo Group seems set to buy back that company, known as Global Solutions, giving them back the contract that had been taken away because of the kind of abuses described in Section 3. Such maneuvers, deliberately intended to confuse and make investigations difficult, are now being tracked by the Service Employees International Union, a 1.6 million-member security officers union, and posted to a website (http://www.focusonGroup4Falck.com). The Geo Group forecasts even more rapid growth in 2004 for the self-proclaimed "global leader in outsourcing," including its security operations at many US nuclear power stations, which are the subject of considerable controversy. This rosy prediction is not surprising given the ongoing expansion of the privatization, or outsourcing, of the war in Iraq. An analysis in the *New York Times* (April 19, 2004, A1) suggests that the private security firms were originally budgeted to receive some 10 percent of the $18 billion specifically allocated by Congress for reconstructing the Iraqi infra-structure as part of the total $87 billion package authorized for security and reconstruction in Iraq. With the continuing crisis, and the consequent ability of the private firms to bill up to $1500 a day for each person's services, this figure has risen to an astonishing 25 percent, that is to say, $4.5 billion. Figures like these make it clear why the flow of American money has failed to significantly improve living conditions for ordinary Iraqis, even as we are told that oil production has now exceeded pre-war levels. Hints abound that still more funds for military purposes will be required. From this point, it seems likely that a sequence of undesirable consequences is likely to follow. On the one hand, the notional transfer of sovereignty in June will not be accompanied by one of power, which will remain in the hands of the US-led Coalition. At the same time, while the sheer firepower of the US army will no doubt suppress individual moments of insurrection like the current one, the long-term pattern seems set as a replay of such struggles as the war for liberation in Algeria. Indeed, Pentagon planners recently had their staff watch Gillo Pontecorvo's 1965 classic film *The Battle of Algiers* as a model of how to win the war on terrorism while losing the hearts and minds of the people. If Algeria is the model, then that country's subsequent history of Islamic resistance to the Front Liberation Nationale (FLN), culminating in the suppressed elections of 1991 and the violent civil war that followed, is a grim warning. From the anti-war perspective, there is little to cheer here, as Iraq does not have a progressive liberation force equivalent to the FLN or Vietcong. It seems that in the hypertime of globalization, we simply cut to the chase, like today's special effects dominated action movies.

Of course, *The Battle of Algiers* was notable above all for its evocation of the French use of torture as a means of obtaining information, the indispensable element in counter-insurrection warfare. Interrogation centers at Bagram in Afghanistan or at Baghdad International Airport, have been more or less openly using procedures amounting to torture. Their activities have been documented by organizations like Amnesty International and Human Rights Watch without creating a significant stir in Western media and political circles. Indeed, at the end of April, Michael Ignatieff published an essay in the *New York Times*, justifying "limited" torture. As so often, the model here is Israel, where torture can be justified if the interrogators are trying to save lives. It is of course hard to imagine the regime that would feel it could not use this defence. Ignatieff himself gets tied into logical knots. He claims that sleep deprivation should be allowed but that prisoners should be allowed "essential rest." These two goals are not compatible. Nor does it make sense to outlaw "physical coercion or abuse" while permitting "disinformation and disorientation" if you know, as Ignatieff does, that "those who are tortured stay tortured for ever."[4] Mental stress and the experience of being "broken" are the essence of torture: the choice of physical or psychological method is a refinement of the torturer. It was no doubt bad luck for Ignatieff that his essay appeared at the same moment that photographs of torture were published by the television show *60 Minutes II* in the US. Given that it was common knowledge that this torture was being practiced, Ignatieff cannot claim ignorance. But what could not have been predicted was the childish glee with which the American reservists were seen carrying out the humiliation of their Iraqi prisoners. The relaxed postures of the prison guards in the photographs – and the fact that they engaged in photography at all – attest to the long-standing nature of the practices being depicted. For all the shocking news value of these photographs, they have a very old genealogy. Edward Said has documented that medieval Christianity held Mohammed responsible for "lechery, debauchery, sodomy, and a whole battery of assorted treacheries."[5] So in subjecting Iraqi prisoners to a range of sexualized punishment and in egregiously punishing the minor violation of theft, the Coalition were acting out a centuries-old pattern of latent Orientalism. In their ribald laughter and sexualized overtones, these photographs evoke the terrible postcards made at the scenes of lynchings in early twentieth-century America. The revived use of Abu Ghraib, Saddam's former prison and torture center, displays the most cynical form of neo-colonial reason, when the only remaining justification for the invasion was to close the torture rooms. Indeed, Fallujah has been returned to the control of a Republican guard general as if the Marines have suddenly become students of Baudrillard, determined to show that the war never happened after all. It should finally be emphasized that what happened at Abu Ghraib was a direct consequence of the reactionary globalization promoted by the empire of camps. Indeed, it was the arrival in Iraq of Major General Geoffrey Miller from the camp at Guantánamo Bay in August 2003 that spurred the change at Abu Ghraib from detention to the unrestrained pursuit of interrogation. Participating in that interrogation were members of private contracting firms such as CACI International and Titan Inc., together with American corrections officers who were experienced in the sexualized modes of humiliating prisoners commonplace in US prisons. When this private and public prison empire was blended with military interrogation techniques, the consequence was the refined torture technique known as the "Vietnam," in which a hooded prisoner standing on a box connected to wires was led to believe he would be electrocuted if he stepped off. This mode of torture used to be preferred precisely because it left no visible marks but the digital cameras and computers that were so central to the success of the US-led invasion have now "blown back" the sight of Americans as torturers. While none of this is new, its encapsulation in a visual image changes the dynamics of the invisibility of the empire of camps.

After the emergence of these images, it seems possible to envisage an end to the empire of camps. Just as decolonization was pursued by legal and international means as well as resistance struggles, evoked by the importance of the United Nations in *The Battle of Algiers*, so must the refusal of this empire be as international as possible. At the end of this month the US Supreme Court heard a series of cases contesting the internment of individuals without habeas corpus at Guantánamo Bay and the designation of US citizens as enemy combatants. A further case will decide whether the administration is entitled to what it calls a "zone of autonomy" in its policies, specifically Vice-President Cheney's energy commission. In short, the administration claims to be beyond oversight. It is possible that the Court will decide against the administration simply because it likes to be seen as the arbiter of all such matters. It is noticeable that supra-national legal and political institutions are in a good deal of trouble these days. The US refuses to submit its officials and soldiers to the authority of the International Criminal Court of Human Rights in the Hague (one issue on which it agreed with Saddam Hussein's Iraq), even as American companies are finding that they can win cases in domestic courts only to have them appealed to NAFTA tribunals. Many European nations are submitting the new European Constitution to a referendum that may well lead to the collapse of the project. Contesting the empire of camps might well mean an unglamorous assertion of the importance of such international justice. Unpopular with left and right for different reasons, such internationalism could be central to the "medium theory" of the "radical center" proposed by W.J.T. Mitchell, following the model proposed by the Czech playwright and novelist Karel Capek in the 1930s.[6] If the "radical center" has unfortunate echoes with the New Labour party of Tony Blair, it also recalls the success of the Charter 88 movement in pushing for constitutional reform of Britain's antiquated governance structures. Such changes as the abolition of the hereditary principle in the House of Lords and Scottish and Welsh devolution are among the most positive achievements of the 1997 Labour government. Charter 88 was itself modeled on the

Czechoslovakian organization Charter 77, set up by a group of dissidents including the playwright and future Czech president Vaclav Havel. Their insistence on observing the text of the 1975 Helsinki Agreement and other previously ignored constitutions and conventions was a key contributor to the collapse of the Soviet bloc in 1989–91, an event that seemed improbable right up until the moment it was happening.

On this model, a global reform movement could take its cue, as Paul Gilroy has suggested, from a re-examination of the United Nations charters of the 1940s. Such texts as the UN Convention on Genocide,[7] for example, are remarkable in their breadth of vision. Under the Convention, for example, it is painfully obvious that the Clinton administration's prevarications about the whether the events in Rwanda that took place ten years ago this month constituted a genocide were a flagrant denial of the terms of the Convention.[8] Article 2 simply states: "Genocide means any of the following acts committed with intent to destroy, in whole or in part, a national, ethnical, racial or religious group as such: (a) Killing members of the group." What is also clear is that making a genuine commitment to the letter and the spirit of this and other conventions already recognized as law would entail nothing less than a revolution of governance. For example, if, as Article 2 Section E states, genocide is "forcibly transferring children of the group to another group," then there is no question that the Australian policy of transferring Aboriginal children to white families – the Stolen Generation, as they are known – was genocide. Each section in this book ended with a hopeful or even utopian gesture. So perhaps it would be fitting to end this note with the most utopian idea of all: that international human rights law be adhered to by its contracting parties. Such a Charter 04 movement might have little immediate impact on the ground in Iraq but might prevent future pre-emptive conflicts from being pursued. The specter of justice is perhaps the hardest of all to see, let alone to speak to.[9]

New York
April 30, 2004.

Notes and references

Prologue: Babylonian modernity

1   W.J.T. Mitchell, *Picture Theory* (Chicago: University of Chicago Press, 1994), p. 16.

2   Sarat Maharaj, "Perfidious Fidelity: The Untranslatability of the Other," in Sarah Campbell and Gilane Tawadros (eds), *Modernity and Difference* (London: Institute of International Visual Arts, 2001), p. 33.

3   See Matthew Arnold, *Culture and Anarchy*, ed. Samuel Lipman (New Haven and London: Yale University Press, [1869] 1994), pp. 87–95.

4   See Zadie Smith, *The Autograph Man* (London and New York: Hamish Hamilton, 2002) and Leon Wieseltier, *Kaddish* (New York: Knopf, 1998).

5   "Gilgamesh," in *Myths from Mesopotamia*, translated with an introduction and notes by Stephanie Dalley (Oxford: Oxford University Press, 2000), p. 50.

6   Jacques Derrida, "Des Tours de Babel," in Peggy Kamuf (ed.), *A Derrida Reader. Between The Blinds* (New York: Columbia University Press, 1991), p. 244.

7   Stuart Hall, "Cultural Identity and Diaspora," in Nicholas Mirzoeff (ed.), *Diaspora and Visual Culture: Representing Africans and Jews* (London and New York: Routledge, 2000), p. 26.

8   Edward Said, "A window on the world," *Guardian* (1 August, 2003), accessed at http://books.guardian.co.uk.

9   Michael Hardt and Antonio Negri, *Empire* (Cambridge MA and London: Harvard University Press, 2000), pp. 31–34.

10 Michel Foucault, "Truth and Power" (1976), in James D. Faubion (ed.), Robert Hurley *et al.* (trans.), *Power* (New York: New Press, 2000), p. 116.

11   Susan Buck-Morss, *Thinking Past Terror: Islamism and Critical Theory on the Left* (New York: Verso, 2003), pp. 21–38.

12   Buck-Morss, *Thinking Past Terror*, p. 29.

13   Jacques Derrida, *On Cosmopolitanism and Forgiveness*, trans. Mark Dooley and Michael Hughes, preface by Simon Critchley and Richard Kearney (London and New York: Routledge, 2001), p. 17.

14   Louis Althusser, *Essays on Ideology* (London: Verso, 1984), p. 48.

15   Jacques Rancière, from *Aux bords de la politique* (Paris, 1998), p. 177; quoted by Kristin Ross, *May '68 and its Afterlives* (Chicago: University of Chicago Press, 2002), pp. 22–23.

16   Stuart Hall, "Then and Now: a Re-evaluation of the New Left," (1989), quoted by James Clifford, "Taking Identity Politics Seriously: 'The Contradictory, Stony Ground . . .'," in Paul Gilroy, Lawrence Grossberg and Angela McRobbie (eds), *Without Guarantees: In Honour of Stuart Hall* (London: Verso, 2000), p. 94.

17   Naomi Klein, "The Year of the Fake," *The Nation* (January 26, 2004), p. 10.

18   Emerson to Carlyle, March 31, 1837, quoted by Albert J. Lavally, *Carlyle and the Idea of the Modern: Studies in Carlyle's Prophetic Literature and its Relation to Blake, Nietzsche, Marx and others* (New Haven and London: Yale University Press, 1968), p. 12.

19   Mogens Trolle Larsen, *The Conquest of Assyria* (New York: Routledge, 1996), p. 358.

20   See Zainab Bahrani, "History in Reverse: Archaeological Illustration and the Invention of Assyria," pp. 15–28; ibid., "Conjuring Mesopotamia: Imaginative geography and a world past," in Lynn Meskel (ed.), *Archaeology Under Fire: Nationalism, politics and heritage in the Eastern Mediterranean and Middle East* (London: Routledge, 1998), pp. 159–74; Frederick N. Bohrer, "Inventing Assyria: Exoticism and Reception in Nineteenth-Century England and France," *The Art Bulletin* LXXX (June 1998), pp. 336–56.

21   See Miriam Hansen, *Babel and Babylon: Cinema and Spectatorship* (Cambridge MA: Harvard University Press, 1991).

22   Edmund Gosse, *Father and Son*, (New York: WW Norton, [1907] 1963), p. 59.

23   Quoted by Barry Hankins, *Uneasy in Babylon: Southern Baptist Conservatives and American Culture* (Tuscaloosa and London: University of Alabama Press, 2002),p. 62.

24   Sandra Mackey, *The Reckoning: Iraq and the Legacy of Saddam Hussein* (New York and London: WW Norton, 2002), p. 37.

25   Oscar Wilde, "Ireland and the Irish During the Latter Half of the Eighteenth Century," in *The Prose of Oscar Wilde* (New York: Bonibooks,

1935), p. 530; also quoted by Julia Prewitt Brown, *Cosmopolitan Criticism: Oscar Wilde's Philosophy of Art* (Charlottesville and London: University Press of Virginia, 1997), p. 25.

26 Edward Wilmot Blyden, "The Jewish Question," in Hollis R. Lynch (ed.), *Black Spokesman: Selected Published Writings of Edward Wilmot Blyden* (New York: Humanities Press, 1971), pp. 209–14.

27 Dipesh Chakrabarty, *Provincializing Europe: Postcolonial Thought and Historical Difference* (Princeton NJ: Princeton University Press, 2000), p. 83.

28 Paul Gilroy, "Diaspora, utopia and the critique of capitalism," in his *"There Ain't No Black in the Union Jack": The Cultural Politics of Race and Nation* (Chicago: University of Chicago Press, 1991), p. 188. See pp. 153–222 for an extensive discussion.

29 Manuel Castells, *The Network Society* (Oxford: Blackwell, 1996).

30 Gerschom Scholem, *Walter Benjamin: The Story of a Friendship*, trans. Harry Zohn (New York: New York Review Books, 2001), p. 103.

31 Emma Goldman, *Anarchism and Other Essays* (New York: Dover, [1917] 1969), pp. 49 and 55. She was referring to Wilde's *Soul of Man under Socialism* (1891) for which see Jeff Nunokawa, "The Protestant Ethic and the Spirit of Anorexia: The Case of Oscar Wilde," in his *Tame Passions of Wilde: The Styles of Manageable Desire* (Princeton: Princeton University Press, 2003), pp. 90–120.

32 Jacques Derrida, *Spectres of Marx* (New York: Routledge, 1994).

33 Geert Lovink, "The Twlight of the Digerati," *Dark Fiber* (Cambridge MA: MIT Press, 2002), pp. 1–22.

Section 1: Babylon, Long Island

1 Donna Haraway, *Simians, Cyborgs, and Women: The Reinvention of Nature* (New York: Routledge, 1991), p. 188.

2 Robert Blair St. George, *Conversing By Signs: Poetics of Implication in Colonial New England Culture* (Chapel Hill NC and London: University of North Carolina Press, 1998), p. 7, hereinafter *CBS*.

3 See Anne Friedberg, *Window Shopping* (Berkeley: University of California Press, 1995); Anna McCarthy, *Ambient Television* (Durham NC: Duke University Press, 2001); Irit Rogoff, *Terra Infirma: Geography and Visual Culture* (London and New York: Routledge, 2000).

4 McCarthy, *Ambient Television*; see also Toby Miller, *Technologies of Truth: Cultural Citizenship and the Popular Media* (Minneapolis: University of Minnesota Press, 1998), p. 57.

5 Judith Halberstam, "The Transgender Gaze in *Boys Don't Cry*," in Nicholas Mirzoeff (ed.), *The Visual Culture Reader*, second edition (London and New York: Routledge, 2002), pp. 669–73.

6   For details, see the brilliant essay by Jonathan L. Beller, "Kino-I, Kino-World: Notes on the Cinematic Mode of Production," in Mirzoeff (ed.), *The Visual Culture Reader*, pp. 60–85.

7   Jerry Saltz,, "Kara Walker: Ill-will and Desire," *Flash Art* (November/December 1996), pp. 82–86.

8   *CBS*, p. 9.

9   James B. Cooper, "Babylon," in *History of Suffolk County, New York* (New York: W.W. Munsell and Co., 1882), p. 30.

10   Nell Irvin Painter, *Sojourner Truth: A Life, A Symbol* (New York: WW Norton, 1996), pp. 82–83.

11   *The Narrative of Sojourner Truth*, ed. Margaret Washington (New York: Vintage Classics, 1993), pp. 82–83.

12   Guy Debord, "Theory of the Dérive," in Libero Andreotti and Xavier Costa (eds), *Theory of the Dérive and other Situationist Writings on the City* (Barcelona: ACTAR, 1996), p. 22.

13   All Hummer facts from *New York Times* April 5, 2003, C14.

14   Jurgen Habermas, *The Structural Transformation of the Bourgeois Public Sphere* (Cambridge MA: MIT Press, [1962] 1989), pp. 43 and 51.

15   Quoted in Steven Holtzman, *Digital Mosaics: The Aesthetics of Cyberspace* (New York: Simon and Schuster, 1997), p. 183.

16   Constance L. Hays, "Grocer's Strategy: Be What Wal-Mart is Not," *New York Times* (August 20, 2003), C1 and C6.

17   "The Wal-Martization of America," *New York Times* (November 15, 2003), A12.

18   See Friedberg, *Window Shopping*; Lori Anne Loeb, *Consuming Angels: Advertising and Victorian Women* (New York: Oxford University Press, 1994); and Ann Bermingham, "Elegant females and gentleman connoisseurs. The commerce in culture and self-image in eighteenth-century England," in Bermingham and John Brewer (eds), *The Consumption of Culture 1600–1800, Image, Object, Text* (London and New York: Routledge, 1995).

19   Samuel R. Delaney, *Times Square Red, Times Square Blue* (New York: NYU Press, 1999).

20   See David Halle, *Inside Culture: Art and Class in the American Home* (Chicago: University of Chicago Press, 1993), p. 29ff.

21   Eyal Weizman, "Ariel Sharon and the Geometry of Occupation," open-democracy.net (8 September, 2003), p. 7.

22   Gaynell Stone, "Long Island as America: A New Look at the First Inhabitants," *Long Island Historical Journal*, vol. 1 no. 2 (Spring 1989), p. 162.

23   Richard P. Harmond and Geoffrey L. Rossano, "Long Island as America," *Long Island Historical Journal*, vol. 1 no. 1 (Fall 1988), p. 4.

24 "Outline History of the State of New York," (author anon.) in *History of Suffolk County, New York*, p. 15.

25 Frank J. Cavaioli, "The Ku Klux Klan on Long Island," *Long Island Forum* 42 (May 1979), pp. 100–106.

26 *CBS*, p. 93.

27 *CBS*, p. 36.

28 *CBS*, p. 159.

29 *CBS*, p. 126.

30 Halle, *Inside Culture*, pp. 49–51.

31 Weizman, "Ariel Sharon and the Geometry of Occupation," Part Two, opendemocracy.net (September 10, 2003), p. 2.

32 Judith Halberstam, *Skin Shows: Gothic Horror and the Technology of Monsters* (Durham NC: Duke University Press, 1995), p. 162.

33 Slavoj Zizek, "Welcome to the Desert of the Real," at http://lacan.com/desertsym.htm, accessed 9/8/03.

34 Quoted by Tony Williams, "Is the Devil an American? William Dieterle's *The Devil and Daniel Webster*," in Alain Silver and James Ursini (eds), *The Horror Film Reader* (New York: Limelight Editions, 2000), p. 144.

35 Halberstam, *Skin Shows*, p. 21.

36 Karl Marx, *On the Jewish Question,* in *Early Writings*, ed. and trans. T.B. Bottomore (New York: McGraw-Hill, [1844] 1963), p. 38.

37 Halberstam, *Skin Shows*, p. 100.

38 Jon Katz, *Geeks: How Two Lost Boys Rode the Internet Out of Idaho* (New York: Villard, 2000), p. 163.

39 See Roger Wunderlich, "Modern Times," PhD dissertation, SUNY Stony Brook, 1977.

40 *Fantastic!*, curated by Nato Thompson, Massachussetts Museum of Contemporary Art, North Adams, MA, 2002.

41 See T.J. Clark, *Farewell to an Idea: Episodes from a History of Modernism* (New Haven and London: Yale University Press, 1999), p. 103; and Sarat Maharaj, "Xeno-Epistemics: Makeshift Kit for Sounding Visual Art as Knowledge Production and the Retinal Regimes," in *Documenta 11 Platform 5: The Exhibition* (Ostfildern-Ruit [Germany]: Hatje Cantze Publishers, 2002), pp. 71–84.

42 See Peter Kropotkin, *The Conquest of Bread and Other Writings*, ed. Marshall S. Shatz (Cambridge: Cambridge University Press, 1995); Emma Goldman, *Anarchism and Other Essays* (New York: Dover Publications, 1969); and Kropotkin, *In Russian and French Prisons* (London: Ward and Downey, 1887).

43 These connections evoke the wonderful book by Greil Marcus, *Lipstick Traces: A secret history of the twentieth century* (Cambridge MA: Harvard University Press, 1990).

44 Peter Kropotkin, *Memoirs of a Revolutionist* (Boston and New York: Houghton Mifflin, 1930), p. 216. Cited without reference by Eric S. Raymond, "The Cathedral and the Bazaar," at http://firstmonday. dk/issues/issue3_3/raymond/ accessed on 10/13/03.

45 J. Huizinga, *Homo Ludens* (London: Routledge, Kegan, Paul, [1940] 1980), p. 8.

46 Constant, "Unitary Urbanism" (1960), rpr. Mark Wigley, *Constant's New Babylon: The Hyperarchitecture of Desire* (Roterdam: Witte de With/010 Publishers, 1998), p. 133.

47 Constant, "New Babylon: Outline of a Culture," written 1960–65, rpr. in Wigley, *Constant's New Babylon*, p. 160.

48 Peter Wollen, "Bitter Victory: The Art of the Situationist International," in Elizabeth Sussmann (ed.), *on the Passage of a few people through a rather brief moment in time: The Situationist International 1957–72* (Cambridge MA: MIT Press, 1991), p. 45.

49 Constant, unpublished lecture of 1964, quoted in Wigley, *Constant's New Babylon*, p. 13.

50 Quoted by Andrew Hussey, *The Game of War: The Life and Death of Guy Debord* (London: Pimlico Press, 2002), p. 47.

51 Greil Marcus, "Guy Debord's *Mémoires*: A Situationist Primer," in Sussmann (ed.), *on the Passage of a few people through a rather brief moment in time*, p. 127.

52 Hussey, *The Game of War*, p. 147.

53 Norbert Wiener, *God and Golem, Inc.* (Cambridge MA: MIT Press, 1965), p. 95.

54 Wiener, *God and Golem*, pp. 49–50.

Section 2: The banality of images

1 Arthur Conan Doyle, "The Silver Blaze," in *The Complete Sherlock Holmes Short Stories* (London: John Murray, 1928).

2 Guy Debord, *The Society of the Spectacle* (New York: Zone, 1991), p. 32.

3 "Technology and Utopia," held at the Humanities Institute, SUNY Stony Brook, March 2000. See www.stonybrook.edu/humanities.

4 Ernst Mandel, *Late Capitalism*, trans. Joris de Bres (London: Verso, 1975), pp. 274–309.

5 See Patrick Wright, *Tank* (London: Faber and Faber, 2000) for a brilliant analysis of the history of the tank, which inspired these thoughts.

6 Allan Sekula, "The Body and the Archive," *October* (1986).

7 Sources on the fighting at al-Hillah include: "Red Cross: Civilians killed in Apache attack," Associated Press report posted at www.military

city.com/iraq/1733329.html; Bill Reynolds with AFP and AP material, "Massacre in Babylon," www.sf-frontlines.com/print.php?sid=150; Bill Duryea, "Media: French, US papers treat bombing toll differently," http://seattlepi.nwsource.com/national/115784_media04.shtml; "Battle Update," *Sydney Morning Herald*, www.smh.com.au/articles/2003/04/021048962792593.html; translated reports from the Russian site iraqwar.ru posted at www.aeronautics.ru/news/news 002/news086.htm; and at www.aeronautics.ru/news/news002/iraq war_ru_019.htm; *New York Times* April 1–7, 2003. All sites accessed 04/09/03.

8   W.G. Sebald, *On the Natural History of Destruction* (New York: Random House, 2003), p. 98.

9   Alan Bennett, "Diary of a Shameful Year," *London Review of Books* (8 January, 2004), entry for 10 April, 2003, p. 5.

10 Zainab Bahrani, "Iraq's Cultural Heritage: Monuments, History, and Loss," *Art Journal* (Winter 2003), p. 17.

11 Sigmund Freud, *Beyond the Pleasure Principle*, introduction by Peter Gay, trans. James Strachey (New York: WW Norton, 1961), p. 59.

12 Sigmund Freud, "The Uncanny," *Standard Edition of the Complete Psychological Works of Sigmund Freud*, ed. and trans. by James Strachey, vol. XVII (London: The Hogarth Press, 1955), p. 234.

13 Toby Manhire, "Arab Press Review," guardian.co.uk 12/17/03, accessed same day.

14 Walter Benjamin, *Illuminations* (New York: Shocken, 1968), p. 84. Observant readers might recall that I have used this quotation in another book, *Bodyscape*, which centered on the changes in perceiving the body in postmodern art and culture. It seems a world ago, but it was only eight years.

15 Freud, *Beyond the Pleasure Principle*, p. 78.

16 Walter Benjamin, *The Arcades Project*, trans. Howard Eiland and Kevin McLaughlin (Cambridge MA and London: Belknap Press of Harvard University Press, 1999), p. 90.

17 *New York Times* (May 12, 2003), C6.

18 Benjamin, *Illuminations*, p. 89.

19 See Zainab Bahrani, *The Graven Image: Representation in Babylonia and Assyria* (Philadelphia: University of Pennsylvania Press, 2003).

20 Donald P. Hansen, "Art of the Akkadian Dynasty," in Joan Aruz and Roland Wallefels (eds), *Art of the First Cities* (New Haven and London: Yale University Press, 2003), p. 190.

21 Zainab Bahrani, *Women of Babylon: Gender and Representation in Mesopotamia* (London and New York: Routledge, 2001), p. 159.

22   Cuneiform tablet, cat no. 322c, *Art of the First Cities*, p. 459.

23   Neal Stephenson, *Snow Crash* (New York: Bantam Books, 1992), p. 398.

24   Gary Shapiro, *Archaeologies of Vision: Foucault and Nietzsche on Seeing and Saying* (Chicago: University of Chicago Press, 2003), p. 160.

25   *Arcades*, p. 116.

26   See Gerschom Scholem, *Walter Benjamin: The Story of a Friendship*, trans. Harry Zohn (New York: New York Review of Books, 2001), p. 162.

27   Miriam Hansen, *Babel and Babylon: Spectatorship in American Silent Film* (Chicago: University of Chicago Press, 1991), p. 174.

28   Cotton Mather, cited by Robert Blair St. George, *Conversing by Signs: Poetics of Implication in Colonial New England Culture* (Chapel Hill NC and London: University of North Carolina Press, 1998), p. 123.

29   Ralph Waldo Emerson, quoted by Mikhail Iampolski, *The Memory of Tiresias: Intertextuality and Film* (Berkeley: University of California Press, 1998), p. 117. See also Iampolski's fascinating discussion of *Intolerance*, pp. 107–21.

30   Quoted by Mrs. Rich, in her "Introduction" to Claudius James Rich, *Narrative of a Journey to the Site of Babylon in 1811*, edited by Mrs. Rich (London: Duncan and Malcolm, 1839), xxviii n.

31   Rich, *Narrative*, p. 96.

32   See http://www.warsawvoice.pl, accessed 9/8/2003.

33   *New York Times*, March 27, 2003, B12.

34   Quoted by Edward Said, *Orientalism* (New York: Viking, 1978), p. 38.

35   Quoted by Mogens Trolle Larsen, *The Conquest of Assyria: Excavations in an Antique Land* (London: Routledge, 1994), p. 95.

36   Rich, p. 102.

37   Rich, p. 99.

38   A. Leo Oppenheim, *Ancient Mesopotamia: Portrait of a Dead Civilization*, revised edition completed by Erica Reiner (Chicago: University of Chicago Press, 1977), pp. 324–27.

39   Joe Sacco, *Palestine* (Seattle: Fantagraphics Books, 2001).

40   Marjane Satrapi, *Persepolis* (New York: Pantheon Books, 2003), p. 41.

41   Satrapi, *Persepolis*, p. 102.

42   Satrapi, *Persepolis*, p. 116.

43   Art Spiegelman, *In the Shadow of No Towers*, *London Review of Books* (August 7, 2003), vol. 25 no. 15, pp. 20–21.

44   This debate has been extensively discussed by Miriam Hansen in her essays "Of Mice and Ducks: Benjamin and Adorno on Disney," *South Atlantic Quarterly* 92, no. 1 (January 1993), pp. 27–61; and "Benjamin and Cinema: Not A One-Way Street," *Critical Inquiry* 25, no. 2 (winter 1003), pp. 306–43. See also Esther Leslie, *Hollywood Flatlands* (London: Verso, 2003).

45 Walter Benjamin, "Mickey Mouse," (1931) in Michael W. Jennings, Howard Eiland and Gary Smith (eds), *Selected Writings, Vol. 2 1927–34* (Cambridge MA: Belknap Press of Harvard University Press, 1999), p. 545.
46 *Arcades*, p. 114.

Section 3: The empire of camps

1 Paget Henry, quoted by Ennis Barrington Edmonds, *Rastafari* (New York and Oxford: Oxford University Press, 2003), p. 50. See his chapter "Babylon and Dread Revitalization," pp. 41–66, for a full genealogy of the concept.
2 Quoted in Edmonds, *Rastafari*, p. 44.
3 Stuart Hall, "Cultural Identity and Diaspora," in Nicholas Mirzoeff (ed.), *Diaspora and Visual Culture: Representing Africans and Jews* (London and New York: Routledge, 2000), p. 29.
4 Michel Foucault, *Discipline and Punish: The Birth of the Prison*, trans. Alan Sheridan (New York: Pantheon, 1977).
5 Manuel Castells, "The Net and the Self: Working Notes for a Critical Theory of the Information Society," in Peter Weibel and Timothy Druckery (eds), *Net condition: art and global media* (Cambridge MA and London: MIT Press, 2001), pp. 34–35.
6 Antonio Negri and Michael Hardt, *Empire* (Cambridge MA: Harvard University Press, 2000), p. 60.
7 Achille Mbembe, "Necropolitics," *Public Culture* 15:1 (Winter 2003), p. 34.
8 John Upton. "In the streets of Londonistan," *London Review of Books*, vol. 26 no. 2 (January 2004), pp. 6–8.
9 Paul N. Edwards, *The Closed World: Computers and the Politics of Discourse in Cold War America* (Cambridge MA and London: MIT Press, 1996), p. 307.
10 Edwards, *The Closed World*, p. 341.
11 See Peter Kropotkin, *In Russian and French Prisons* (London: Ward and Downey, 1887), p. 358.
12 See Peter Kropotkin, *Memoirs of a Revolutionist* (Boston and New York: Houghton Mifflin, 1930), p. 51.
13 Janet Semple, *Bentham's Prison* (Oxford: Clarendon Press, 1993), p. 103.
14 Ibid., p. 100.
15 Foucault, *Discipline and Punish*, p. 206.
16 Thomas C. Holt, *The Problem of Freedom: Race, Labor, and Politics in Jamaica and Britain, 1832–1938* (Baltimore and London: Johns Hopkins University Press, 1992), pp. 105–7.

17 Catherine Hall, *Civilizing Subjects: Metropole and Colony in the English Imagination 1830–1867* (Chicago: University of Chicago Press, 2002), p. 23.

18 Quoted by Holt, *The Problem of Freedom*, p. 303.

19 Holt, *The Problem of Freedom*, pp. 300 and 127.

20 Foucault, *Discipline and Punish*, p. 201.

21 Semple, *Bentham's Prison*, pp. 116–20.

22 Wolfgang Schivelbusch, *Disenchanted Night: The Industrialization of Light in the Nineteenth Century*, trans. Angela Davies (Berkeley and London: University of California, 1988), p. 26.

23 See Suvendrini Perera, "What is a Camp . . .?," *borderlands*, vol. no 1, 2002, paragraph 9, at www.borderlandsejournal.adelaide.edu.au.

24 Perera, "What is a Camp . . .?", paragraph 18.

25 Thomas Carlyle, "Model Prisons," in *Latter-Day Pamphlets* (London: Chapman Hall 1855), p. 14.

26 From *The London*, 12 March, 1896, accessed on-line at www.davidric. dircon.co.uk/survunfi.html on 5/22/01.

27 Semple, *Bentham's Prison*, p. 132.

28 Semple, *Bentham's Prison*, p. 16.

29 Figures from Leslie Fairweather, *Prison Architecture: Policy, Design and Experience* (London: Architectural Press, 2001), quoted by Jonathan Glancey, "Within these walls," *Guardian*, February 1, 2001.

30 *New York Times*, April 7, 2003, A12, and July 28, 2003, A12.

31 See Manuel Castells, *The Rise of the Network Society* (Oxford: Blackwell, 1996).

32 Arjun Appadurai, "The Heart of Whiteness," *Callaloo* 16:4 (1993), p. 803.

33 Quoted by Frank Owen, "Let Them Eat Software," *Village Voice* (February 6, 1996), p. 31.

34 Susan Buck-Morss, *Dreamworld and Catastrophe: The Passing of Mass Utopia in East and West* (Cambridge MA and London: MIT Press, 2000), p. 3.

35 See especially Giorgio Agamben, *Homo Sacer: Sovereign Power and Bare Life*, trans. Daniel Heller-Roazen (Stanford CA: Stanford University Press, 1998).

36 M. Strathern, quoted by Nigel Thrift, "Capitalism's Cultural Turn," in *Culture and Economy After the Cultural Turn* (London: Sage Publications, 1999), p. 155.

37 Jonathan L. Beller, "Kino-I, Kino World: Notes on the Cinematic Mode of Production," in Nicholas Mirzoeff (ed.), *The Visual Culture Reader* (London and New York, 2002), pp. 60–85.

38 Quotes from business studies in Thrift, "Capitalism's Cultural Turn," pp. 142–43.

39 Gayatri Spivak, *A Critique of Postcolonial Reason* (Cambridge MA: Harvard University Press, 1999), p. 67.

40 Elissa Braunstein and Gerald Epstein, "Creating international credit rules and the Multilateral Agreement on Investment: What are the alternatives?" in Jonathan Michie and John Grieve Smith (eds), *Global Instability: The political economy of world economic governance* (London: Routledge, 1999), pp. 113–16.

41 See Alan Sinfield, *The Wilde Century: Effeminacy, Oscar Wilde and the Queer Moment* (New York: Columbia University Press, 1994), pp. 1–25.

42 See Siobhan Somerville, *Queering the Color Line* (Durham: Duke University Press, 2000).

43 See Arjun Appadurai, *Modernity at Large* (Minneapolis: University of Minnesota Press, 1996).

44 See Lisa Nakamura, " 'Where do You Want to Go Today?' Cybernetic Tourism, the Internet and Transnationality," in Mirzoeff (ed.), *The Visual Culture Reader*, pp. 255–63.

45 Mary Evans, "The Culture Did It: Comments on the 1997 British General Election," in Larry Ray and Andrew Sayer (eds), *Culture and Economy After the Cultural Turn* (London: Sage, 1999), p. 232.

46 Dan Schiller, *Digital Capitalism: Networking the Global Market System* (Cambridge MA: MIT Press, 1999), p. 71.

47 Quoted by Graham Meikle, *Future Active: Media Activism and the Internet* (New York: Routledge, 2002), p. 107.

48 Posted to CNBC.com Message Boards 4/15/2000 at 1.37am.

49 Posted to CNBC.com Message Boards 4/16/2000 at 8.45am.

50 Toby Miller, *Technologies of Truth* (Minneapolis: University of Minnesota Press, 1998), p. 58.

51 Knight Kiplinger, *World Boom Ahead: Why Business and Consumers will prosper*, (Washington DC: Kiplinger Books, 1998), p. 28.

52 Schiller, *Digital Capitalism*, pp. 38–39.

53 Louis Uchitelle, "Inflation Spreading Beyond Fuel and Energy," *New York Times*, April 15, 2000, C1.

54 Laura M. Holson and Saul Hansell, "The Making of an Internet Bubble," *New York Times*, April 23, 2000, C1, 8.

55 Steve Gilliard, "Between the Lies: Godzilla Market Theory," NetSlaves.com (April 24, 2000).

56 Wendy Hui Kyong Chun, "Othering Space," in Mirzoeff (ed.), *The Visual Culture Reader*, pp. 243–54.

57 Irit Rogoff, *Terra Infirma: Geography and Visual Culture* (New York and London: Routledge, 2000), p. 22.

58 Agamben, *Homo Sacer*. See also Paul Gilroy, *Against Race* (Cambridge MA and London: Harvard University Press, 1999); and Angela Y. Davis, *Are Prisons Obsolete?* (New York: Seven Stories Press, 2003).

59   *New York Times* (May 21, 2003), A22.

60   Patrick Barkham, "No Waltzing in Woomera," *The Guardian Weekend*, May 25, 2002, pp. 24–31.

61   Alison Bashford and Carolyn Strange, "Asylum Seekers and National Histories of Detention," *Australian Journal of Politics and History*, vol. 48 no. 4 (2002), pp. 509–27.

62   Foucault, *Discipline and Punish*, p. 198.

63   See Steven Morris and Rebecca Allison, "Yarl's Wood: tinderbox that sent asylum plans up in flames," *Guardian* (August 16, 2003), accessed 8/19/2003.

64   Joseph Pugliese, "Penal Asylum: Refugees, Ethics, Hospitality," *borderlands e-journal*, vol. 1 no 1, 2002, www.borderlandsejournal.adelaide. edu.au.vol1no1_2002/pugliese.html.

65   Quoted by Nat Hentoff, "Who Made George Bush Our King?," *Village Voice*, (July 30–August 5, 2003), p. 35.

66   Djaffer Ait Aoudia, "Inside Sangatte," *The Observer* (May 26, 2002), p. 14.

67   Chun, "Othering Space," in Mirzoeff (ed.), *The Visual Culture Reader*, pp. 250–52.

68   "Wackenhut Corrections Comments on the Merger of the Wackenhut Corporation with Group 4 Falck," http://www.prnewswire.com/, accessed on 5/30/2002.

69   "Wackenhut Corrections Reports First Quarter Results," http://www. prnewswire.com/, accessed on 5/30/2002.

70   See press release on-line at http://www.prnewswire.com/cgi-bin/stories.pl?ACCT=105&STORY=/www/story/08–07–2003/00 01997160, accessed 9/29/03.

71   *New York Times* (May 1, 2003), A17.

72   George Packer, "After the War," *The New Yorker* (November 24, 2003), p. 72.

73   Dexter Filkins, "Tough New Tactics by U.S. Tighten Grip on Iraqi Towns," *New York Times* (December 7, 2003), A1.

74   Seymour Hersh, "Moving Targets," *New Yorker* (December 15, 2003), p. 48.

75   See Eyal Weizman, "Ariel Sharon and the Geometry of Occupation," opendemocracy.net (September 2003), accessed 10/30/2003.

76   See for example Saskia Sassen, "The Global City: The Denationalizing of Time and Space," in Gerfried Stocker and Christine Schöpf (eds), *Unplugged: Art as the Scene of Global Conflicts*, Ars Electronica 2002 (Ostfildern-Ruit, Germany: Hatje Canz Publishers, 2002), pp. 18–24.

77   *New York Times*, July 29, 2003, A1.

78 Ian Traynor, "The privatisation of war," *The Guardian International* (December 10, 2003), p. 1.

79 Katie Hafner, "Where the Hall Monitor is a Webcam," *New York Times* (February 27, 2003), G1 and G7.

80 *New York Times* (June 27, 2003), rulings A18–19, editorial A26.

81 Cited by Joichi Ito, "Identity and Privacy in a Globalized Community," in *Unplugged*, p. 246.

82 Meikle, *Future Active*, p. 177.

83 Hannah Arendt, "Introduction: Walter Benjamin, 1892–1940," in Walter Benjamin, *Illuminations*, trans. Harry Zohn (New York: Shocken, 1968), p. 18.

84 Achille Mbembe and Janet Roitman, "Figures of the Subject in Times of Crisis," *Public Culture* no. 16 (Winter, 1995), p. 204.

85 Edwards, *The Closed World*, esp. pp. 309–12.

86 Edward Said, "A window on the world," *Guardian* (1 August, 2003), accessed at http://books.guardian.co.uk.

87 Emmanuel Levinas, "Wholly Otherwise," trans. Simon Critchley in Robert Bernasconi and Simon Critchley (eds), *Re-Reading Levinas* (Indianapolis: Indiana University Press, 1991), p. 4.

88 See Michael Jurgs, *Der Kleine Frieden im Grossen Krieg* (Frankfurt: Bertelsmann, 2003).

89 Emmanuel Levinas, "Cities of Refuge," in *Beyond the Verse: Talmudic Readings and Lectures*, trans. Gary D. Mole (Bloomington: Indiana University Press, 1994), pp. 34–52.

90 Jacques Derrida, "On Cosmopolitanism and Forgiveness," trans. Mark Dooley and Michael Hughes, preface by Simon Critchley and Richard Kearney (London and New York: Routledge, 2001), p. 14.

Afterword: Afterimages

1 Ed Harriman, "On the Thunder Run," *London Review of Books* (April 1, 2004), p. 15.

2 Human Rights Watch, *Off Target: The Conduct of the War and Civilian Casualties in Iraq*, http://www.hrw.org/reports2003/usa1203/index.htm.

3 *New York Times*, April 17, 2004, B1.

4 Michael Ignatieff, "Lesser Evils: What it will cost us to succeed in the war on terror," *New York Times Magazine* (May 2, 2004), p. 86.

5 Edward Said, *Orientalism* (New York: Vintage, 1978), p. 62.

6 W.J.T. Mitchell, "Medium Theory," *Critical Inquiry* 30 (Winter 2004), pp. 324–35.

7 The full text is available at: *Convention on the Prevention and Punishment of the Crime of Genocide*, http://www.unhchr.ch/html/menu3/b/p_genoci.htm.

8 It is unfortunately the case that the United Nations has managed to completely obscure the intended clarity of the genocide Convention, spending, for example, fifteen years debating in sub-committee the meaning of the word "aggression."

9 See Jacques Derrida, *Specters of Marx* (New York: Routledge, 1994).

Index